POETRY BOOK
ENGLISH IN UNITS

John G. Fahy

GILL AND MACMILLAN

PREFACE

This anthology was compiled by and large in spite of the distractions of my friends. Nevertheless, grateful thanks to Maire Mac Donagh for her encyclopaedic music knowledge; to Aidan Kennedy, John Morrissey, Jim Howe and John Fitzpatrick, students of Clonkeen College who have expanded and quite probably ruined any musical taste I might have had; to my friend Seamus Hosey of RTE for his help with the record player; to Liz, without whom this volume would have been even more outrageous; to all the artists and photographers, especially Bill Doyle and Karl Grimes; and to all those who gave advice during the preparation of the text. To the students who read this book, I wish enjoyable learning.

John G. Fahy
Clonkeen College, Dublin
December 1990

Published in Ireland by
Gill and Macmillan Ltd
Goldenbridge
Dublin 8
with associated companies throughout the world
© Selections and editorial matter, John G. Fahy 1991
© artwork Gill and Macmillan, 1991
Design and Cover: Design Works, Dublin
Illustrations: Angela Clarke, Susan Cooper and Aidan Dowling
Picture Research: John G. Fahy, Anne-Marie Ehrlich
Print origination in Ireland by Seton Music Graphics Ltd and Litho Studios.

0 7171 1809 6

All rights reserved. No part of this publication
may be copied, reproduced or transmitted in any form
or by any means, without permission of the publishers. Photocopying any part of this
book is illegal

CONTENTS

Anthology

SECTION A Breaking Out
1. Hairstyle — *John Agard* — 2
2. Reckless — *Pete Brown* — 3
3. Child on Top of a Greenhouse — *Theodore Roethke* — 3
4. A Song in the Front Yard — *Gwendolyn Brooks* — 3
5. The Boys of Winter — *Alan Bold* — 4
6. Warning — *Jenny Joseph* — 4
7. She's Leaving Home — *John Lennon and Paul McCartney* — 5
8. Growing Up? — *Wes Magee* — 6

SECTION B Family
9. The Parent — *Ogden Nash* — 8
10. My Sister Betty — *Gareth Owen* — 8
11. Hugger mugger — *Kit Wright* — 9
12. Indifference — *Harry Graham* — 10
13. Appreciation — *Harry Graham* — 10
14. Father — *Harry Graham* — 10
15. L'Enfant Glacé — *Harry Graham* — 10
16. Tragedy — *Harry Graham* — 10
17. To My Mother — *George Barker* — 11
18. Mother of the Groom — *Seamus Heaney* — 12
19. Digging — *Seamus Heaney* — 12
20. The Cage — *John Montague* — 14

SECTION C Decisions and Choices
21. Tich Miller — *Wendy Cope* — 16
22. Truth — *Barrie Wade* — 17
23. Hero — *Mick Gowar* — 17
24. Limbo — *D.M. Thomas* — 19
25. Edible Anecdote No 24 — *Julie O'Callaghan* — 19
26. The Choosing — *Liz Lochhead* — 20
27. High Flight — *John Magee* — 22
28. The Road Not Taken — *Robert Frost* — 23

SECTION D The World Around Us . . . And Beyond

29.	I Wandered Lonely As a Cloud	William Wordsworth	25
30.	Pied Beauty	Gerard Manley Hopkins	26
31.	Parrot	Alan Brownjohn	26
32.	Pigeons	Richard Kell	27
33.	The Battery Hen	Pam Ayres	28
34.	Saint Francis and the Birds	Seamus Heaney	29
35.	The Dog Lovers	Spike Milligan	30
36.	Dog Exercising Man	Keith Bosley	31
37.	Time for the Knife	Brendan Kennelly	32
38.	Diary of a Church Mouse	John Betjeman	33
39.	Sheep	Ted Hughes	34
40.	The Fox	Adrian Mitchell	36
41.	The Tyger	William Blake	38
42.	Fog	Carl Sandburg	39
43.	Rogue Leaf	Derek Mahon	39
44.	March	Patrick Kavanagh	40
45.	Spring	Gerard Manley Hopkins	40
46.	To Autumn	John Keats	41
47.	Winter	L.A.G. Strong	42
48.	Stopping by Woods on a Snowy Evening	Robert Frost	43
49.	The Wood	Derek Mahon	43
50.	The Shell	James Stephens	44
51.	The Trout	John Montague	45
52.	The Song of the Whale	Kit Wright	46
53.	The River God	Stevie Smith	47
54.	The Diviner	Seamus Heaney	48
55.	Like Dolmens Round my Childhood, the Old People	John Montague	49
56.	At the Bomb Testing Site	William Stafford	51
57.	The World is Too Much With Us	William Wordsworth	52
58.	Space Shot	Gareth Owen	53
59.	The Swirling World Stands Still	John Kitching	54
60.	Retired	Iain Crichton Smith	54
61.	Astronaut	Derek Mahon	54
62.	The Beautiful Strangers	James Kirkup	55
63.	E.T.	Jean Kenward	56

SECTION E Love

64.	King of the Kurzel	*Mick Gowar*	58
65.	Girl's Song	*Wilfrid Gibson*	60
66.	He Wishes for the Cloths of Heaven	*W.B. Yeats*	61
67.	First kiss	*Adam Pritchard*	61
68.	Song for a Beautiful Girl Petrol-Pump Attendant on the Motorway	*Adrian Henri*	61
69.	The Passionate Shepherd to His Love	*Christopher Marlowe*	62
70.	The Passionate Astronaut to His Love	*Greg Smenda*	63
71.	The Thickness of Ice	*Liz Loxley*	64
72.	Lady Diamond	*Unknown*	65
73.	Woman is	*Robin Morgan*	66
74.	The Ideal Husband	*Harry Graham*	68
75.	When you are Old	*W.B. Yeats*	68
76.	Gardening Sunday	*Brian Jones*	69
77.	When I'm Sixty-Four	*John Lennon and Paul McCartney*	69
78.	Yesterday	*Patricia Pogson*	70
79.	Shall I compare thee to a Summer's day?	*William Shakespeare*	71
80.	One Day I Wrote Her Name upon the Strand	*Edmund Spenser*	71

SECTION F Birth to Death

81.	Morning Song	*Sylvia Plath*	73
82.	The Baby	*Ogden Nash*	73
83.	Mid-term Break	*Seamus Heaney*	74
84.	The Identification	*Roger McGough*	74
85.	She Dwelt Among the Untrodden Ways	*William Wordsworth*	76
86.	To Waken an Old Lady	*William Carlos Williams*	76
87.	Good	*R.S. Thomas*	77
88.	Death in the Village	*Graham Hough*	78
89.	Let me Die a Youngman's Death	*Roger McGough*	79
90.	Crossing the Bar	*Alfred, Lord Tennyson*	80
91.	Do not go gentle into that good night	*Dylan Thomas*	80
92.	For everything there is a season . . .	*Ecclesiastes 2*	81

SECTION G War

93.	from 'The Táin'	*Translated by Thomas Kinsella*	83
94.	The Burial of Sir John Moore after Corunna	*Charles Wolfe*	84
95.	The Soldier	*Rupert Brooke*	85
96.	An Irish Airman Forsees His Death	*W.B. Yeats*	86
97.	In Flanders Fields	*John McCrea*	86
98.	Dulce et Decorum est	*Wilfred Owen*	87
99.	The General	*Siegfried Sassoon*	88
100.	Military Service	*Elizabeth Jennings*	88
101.	The Hero	*Siegfried Sassoon*	89
102.	Dead German Youth	*C.P.S. Denholm-Young*	89
103.	Killed In Action	*Juliette de Bairacli-Levy*	90
104.	Shells	*Wilfrid Gibson*	91
105.	The Evacuee	*R.S. Thomas*	91
106.	Pigtail	*Tadeusz Różewicz*	92
107.	Even Hitler had a mother	*Herbert Farjeon*	93
108.	Icarus Allsorts	*Roger McGough*	93
109.	Your Attention Please	*Peter Porter*	95

SECTION H Thoughts for Today

110.	Five Ways to Kill a Man	*Edwin Brock*	99
111.	One in Ten	*UB40*	100
112.	Girls in a Factory	*Denis Glover*	100
113.	Film Star	*Ian Serraillier*	101
114.	Adman	*Nigel Gray*	102
115.	Executive	*John Betjeman*	103
116.	Happiness	*Carl Sandburg*	104
117.	Cultivators	*Susan Taylor*	104
118.	In My Country	*Pitika Ntuli*	105
119.	Grandpa	*Paul Chidyausiku*	105
120.	What is a Protestant, Daddy?	*Paul Durcan*	106
121.	From the Irish	*James Simmons*	108
122.	Missionary	*D.M. Thomas*	108
123.	Let It Be	*John Lennon and Paul McCartney*	111
124.	God's Grandeur	*Gerard Manley Hopkins*	112
125.	Desiderata	*Max Ehrmann*	113

SECTION I Taking your Pen for a Walk

126.	Taking My Pen for a Walk	*Julie O'Callaghan*	*117*
127.	One Way of Flying	*James Kirkup*	*118*
128.	I Hear . . .	*Berlie Doherty*	*119*
129.	After English Class	*Jean Little*	*120*
130.	Timely	*Christopher Nolan*	*120*
131.	Poem to be buried in a time capsule	*James Kirkup*	*121*
132.	January to December	*Patricial Beer*	*123*
133.	Pegasus	*Patrick Kavanagh*	*126*
134.	In My Craft or Sullen Art	*Dylan Thomas*	*128*
135.	The Thought-Fox	*Ted Hughes*	*128*
136.	Breakfast with Gerard Manley Hopkins	*Anthony Brode*	*133*
137.	New Improved Sonnet XVIII	*Peter Titheradge*	*133*

*   *   *   *   *

Glossary of Poetic Terms	*136*
Ten Classroom Activities	*139*
Poetry you will enjoy (Bibliography)	*141*
Exploring the Poems	
'Breaking out':	*145*
'Family':	*152*
'Decisions/Choices':	*156*
'The World Around Us . . . and Beyond':	*158*
'Love':	*168*
'Birth to Death':	*173*
'War':	*175*
'Thoughts for Today':	*180*

ACKNOWLEDGMENTS

For permission to reproduce copyright material, grateful acknowledgment is made to the following: John Agard, c/o Caroline Sheldon Literary Agency, for 'Hairstyle'; Faber and Faber Ltd. for 'Child on Top of a Greenhouse' from *The Collected Poems of Theodore Roethke* by Theodore Roethke; Gwendolyn Brooks for 'A Song in Front Yard' from *Blacks* by the same writer, published in 1987 © by the David Company, Chicago; Alan Bold for 'The Boys of Winter'; John Johnson Ltd. for 'Warning' from *Rose in the Afternoon* by Jenny Joseph; EMI Music Publishing for the lyrics of 'She's Leaving Home' 'When I'm Sixty Four' and 'Let it Be' by John Lennon and Paul McCartney; Wes Magee for 'Growing Up?' from *Morning break and other poems* by Wes Magee (C.U.P. 1989); Curtis Brown Ltd. for 'The Parent' and 'The Baby' by Ogden Nash, © 1931 by Ogden Nash; Collins Publishers for 'My Sister Betty' and 'Space Shot' from *Song of the City* by Gareth Owen; Penguin Books Ltd. for 'Hugger mugger' and 'Song of the Whale' by Kit Wright from *Hot Dog and Other Poems* by Kit Wright (Kestrel Books, 1981) © Kit Wright, 1981; Faber and Faber Ltd. for 'To My Mother' from *Collected Poems* by George Barker; Faber and Faber Ltd. for 'Mother of the Groom' from *Wintering Out* by Seamus Heaney and for 'Digging', 'St Francis and the Birds', 'The Diviner' and 'Mid-term Break' from *Death of a Naturalist* by Seamus Heaney; The Gallery Press for 'The Cage', 'The Trout' and 'Like Dolmens Round My Childhood, The Old People' from *New Selected Poems* (1989) by John Montague; Faber and Faber Ltd. for 'Tich Miller' from *Making Cocoa for Kingsley Amis* by Wendy Cope; Oxford University Press for 'Truth' from *Conkers* by Barrie Wade (1989); Collins Publishers for 'Hero' and 'King of the Kurzel' from *So Far So Good* by Mick Gowar; D.M. Thomas for 'Limbo' and 'Missionary'; Julie O'Callaghan for 'Edible Anecdote No 24' and 'Taking My Pen for a Walk'; Polyson for 'The Choosing' from *Dreaming Frankenstein and Collected Poems* by Liz Lochhead; Random Century Group for 'The Road Not Taken' and 'Stopping by Woods on a Snowy Evening' from *The Poetry of Robert Frost* edited by Edward Connery Latham, published by Jonathan Cape © estate of Robert Frost; Alan Brownjohn for 'Parrot'; Random Century for 'Pigeons' from *Differences* by Richard Kell, published by Chatto and Windus; Layston Productions Ltd for 'The Battery Hen' by Pam Ayres, © Pam Ayres; Spike Milligan Productions Ltd. for 'The Dog Lovers' by Spike Milligan; Keith Bosley for 'Dog Exercising Man'; Brendan Kennelly for 'Time for the Knife'; John Murray for 'Diary of a Church Mouse' from *Collected poems* by John Betjeman and 'Executive' from *The Best of Betjeman*; Faber and Faber Ltd. for 'Sheep part 1' and 'The Thought Fox' from *Season Songs* by Ted Hughes; together with 'The Thought Fox' (commentary) from *The Hawk in the Rain* by Ted Hughes; Harcourt Brace Jovanovich Inc. for 'Fog' and 'Happiness' from *Chicago poems* by Carl Sandburg; Derek Mahon for 'Rogue Leaf' and 'Astronaut'; The Gallery Press for 'March' and 'Pegasus' by Patrick Kavanagh'; Methuen for 'Winter' from *The Body's Imperfections* by L.A.C. Strong; Oxford University Press for 'The Wood' from *Derek Mahon – Poems 1962–78* by Derek Mahon; The Society of Authors on behalf of the copyright owner, Mrs Iris Wise for 'The Shell' from *Collected Poems* by James Stephens; James MacGibbons for 'The River God' from *The Collected Poems of Stevie Smith* (Penguin 19th Century Classics); William Stafford for 'At the Bomb Testing Site' from *Stories that Could be True* by William Stafford; John Kitching for 'The Swirling World Stands Still'; Iain Crichton Smith for 'Retired'; James Kirkup for 'The Beautiful Strangers', 'One Way of Flying' and 'Poem to be buried in a Time Capsule'; Jean Kenward for 'E.T.'; Macmillan and Michael Gibson for 'Girl's Song' and 'Shells' from *Collected Poems* by Wilfrid Gibson; Rogers, Coleridge and White for 'Song for a Beautiful Girl Petrol-Pump Attendant on the Motorway' from *Collected Poems* by Adrian Henri; Faber and Faber Ltd. for 'The Thickness of Ice' from *Hard Lines: New Poetry and Prose* by Liz Loxley; Patricia Pogson for 'Yesterday'; Faber and Faber Ltd. for 'Morning Song' from *Ariel* by Sylvia Plath; Random Century Group for 'The Identification', 'Let Me Die a Youngman's Death' and 'Icarus Allsorts' from *Selected Poems* by Roger McGough; Carcanet Press Ltd. for 'To Waken an Old Lady' from *Collected Poems Volume 1* by William Carlos Williams; Gwydion Thomas for 'Good' and 'The Evacuee' by R.S. Thomas; Duckworth for 'Death in the Village' by Graham Hough from *Legends and Pastorals*; David Higham Associates Ltd. for 'Do Not Go Gentle Into That Good Night' and 'In My Craft or Sullen Art' from

(continued inside back cover)

SECTION A
BREAKING OUT

1. HAIRSTYLE
John Agard

What about my hairstyle?
On my head I carry
a phosphorescent porcupine –
but it's mine it's mine
and if you don't like my head
you can drop dead.

What about my hairstyle?
On my head I bear a mane
of flaming dreadlocks
sometimes hidden by the red
    gold and green
but flaming all the same
with I-rie pride of Africa.
Know what I mean?

What about my hairstyle?
On my head I wear
a Mohican rainbow
that makes me glow.
I know some eyebrows go
up in despair
but it's my hair it's my hair.

What about my hairstyle?
On my head I show a crown
of incandescent candy floss.
Who cares if some people frown
and say, 'Young people are lost'.
At least me Mum doesn't get on me back;
she says, 'I suppose you're only young once'.

What about my hairstyle?
On my head I have whispers
of braided beads.
Me Mum says she wouldn't have the patience –
but these beads are in no hurry
I tell them my needs
they listen to the song inside of me.

2. RECKLESS   *Pete Brown*

Last night I was reckless
didn't brush my teeth
and went to bed tasting
my dinner all night

And it tasted good.

3. CHILD ON TOP OF A GREENHOUSE   *Theodore Roethke*

The wind billowing out the seat of my britches,
My feet crackling splinters of glass and dried putty,
The half-grown chrysanthemums staring up like accusers,
Up through the streaked glass, flashing with sunlight,
A few white clouds all rushing eastward,
A line of elms plunging and tossing like horses,
And everyone, everyone pointing up and shouting!

4. A SONG IN THE FRONT YARD   *Gwendolyn Brooks*

I've stayed in the front yard all my life.
I want a peek at the back
Where it's rough and untended and hungry weed grows.
A girl gets sick of a rose.

I want to go in the back yard now
And maybe down the alley,
To where the charity children play.
I want a good time today.

They do some wonderful things.
They have some wonderful fun.
My mother sneers, but I say it's fine
How they don't have to go in at quarter to nine.
My mother, she tells me that Johnnie Mae
Will grow up to be a bad woman.
That George'll be taken to Jail soon or late
(On account of last winter he sold our back gate).

But I say it's fine. Honest, I do.
And I'd like to be a bad woman, too,
And wear the brave stockings of night-black lace
And strut down the streets with paint on my face.

5. THE BOYS OF WINTER   *Alan Bold*

Snow around their boots, they gather
Like an embodiment of the weather:
Huddled there, herded like cattle,
They are animals dressed for battle.
One smokes, another sprawls,
Three of them sloganise the walls,
They look askance at Princes Street
Defiantly in their defeat:
Their breath clouds in the cold.
These young boys, horribly old,
Having nothing (heads shorn of hair).
They do nothing, pollute the air
With verbal debris, have nothing to declare.
They look ahead and blankly stare:
Their eyes are onions of despair.

6. WARNING   *Jenny Joseph*

When I am an old woman I shall wear purple
With a red hat which doesn't go, and doesn't suit me.
And I shall spend my pension on brandy and summer gloves
And satin sandals, and say we've no money for butter.

I shall sit down on the pavement when I'm tired
And gobble up samples in shops and press alarm bells
And run my stick along the public railings
And make up for the sobriety of my youth.
I shall go out in my slippers in the rain
And pick the flowers in other people's gardens
And learn to spit.

You can wear terrible shirts and grow more fat
And eat three pounds of sausages at a go
Or only bread and pickle for a week
And hoard pens and pencils and beermats and
    things in boxes.

But now we must have clothes that keep us dry
And pay our rent and not swear in the street
And set a good example for the children.
We must have friends to dinner and read the papers.

But maybe I ought to practise a little now?
So people who know me are not too shocked
    and surprised
When suddenly I am old, and start to wear
    purple.

7. SHE'S LEAVING HOME

Wednesday morning at five o'clock as the day begins,
Silently closing her bedroom door,
Leaving the note that she hoped would say more.
She goes down stairs to the kitchen clutching her handkerchief,
Quietly turning the back door key,
Stepping outside she is free.
She (*We gave her most of our lives*) is leaving (*Sacrificed most of our
    lives*) home.
(*We gave her everything money could buy*). She's leaving home after
    living alone for so many years.

*John Lennon
and Paul
McCartney*

8. GROWING UP?   *Wes Magee*

It must be, oooh,
a month or more
since they last complained
about the way I eat

or crisps I drop
on the kitchen floor

or not washing my feet

or the TV left on
when I go out

or the spoon clunking
against my teeth

or how loudly I shout

or my unmade bed,
mud on the stair,

soap left to drown
or the state of my hair. . .

It *must* be
a month or more.
Have they given up
in despair?

For years
they've nagged me
to grow up,
to act my age.

Can it be
that it's happened,
that I'm ready
to step out of my cage?

SECTION B
FAMILY

9. THE PARENT *Ogden Nash*

Children aren't happy with nothing to ignore,
And that's what parents were created for.

10. MY SISTER BETTY *Gareth Owen*

My sister Betty said,
'I'm going to be a famous actress.'
Last year she was going to be a missionary.
'Famous actresses always look unhappy but beautiful,'
She said, pulling her mouth sideways
And making her eyes turn upwards
So they were mostly white.
'Do I look unhappy but beautiful?'
'I want to go to bed and read,' I said.
'Famous actresses suffer and have hysterics,' she said.
'I've been practising my hysterics.'
She began going very red and screaming
So that it hurt my ears.
She hit herself on the head with her fists
And rolled off my bed on to the lino.
I stood by the wardrobe where it was safer.
She got up saying, 'Thank you, thank you,'
And bowed to the four corners of my bedroom.
'Would you like an encore of hysterics?' she asked.
'No,' I said from inside the wardrobe.
There was fluff all over her vest.
'If you don't clap enthusiastically,' she said,
I'll put your light out when you're reading.'
While I clapped a bit
She bowed and shouted, 'More, more!'
Auntie Gwladys shouted upstairs,
'Go to bed and stop teasing our Betty.'
'The best thing about being a famous actress,' Betty said,
'Is that you get to die a lot.'
She fell to the floor with a crash
And lay there for an hour and a half

With her eyes staring at the ceiling.
She only went away when I said,
'You really look like a famous actress
Who's unhappy but beautiful.'

When I got into bed and started reading,
She came and switched off my light.
It's not much fun
Having a famous actress for a sister.

11. HUGGER MUGGER   *Kit Wright*

I'd sooner be
Jumped and thumped and dumped,

I'd sooner be
Slugged and mugged . . . than *hugged* . . .

And clobbered with a slobbering
Kiss by my Auntie Jean:

You know what I mean:

Whenever she comes to stay,
You know you're bound

To get one.
A quick
   short
      peck
         would
            be
               OK.
But this is a
Whacking great
Smacking great
Wet one!

All whoosh and spit
And crunch and squeeze
And '*Dear* little boy!'

And 'Auntie's missed you!'
And 'Come to Auntie, she
Hasn't *kissed* you!'
Please don't do it, Auntie,
PLEASE!

Or if you've absolutely
Got to,

And nothing on *earth* can persuade you
Not to,

The trick
Is to make it
Quick,

You know what I mean?

For as things are,
I really would far,

Far sooner be
Jumped and thumped and dumped,

I'd sooner be
Slugged and mugged . . . than *hugged* . . .

And clobbered with a slobbering
Kiss by my Auntie

Jean!

12. Indifference   *Harry Graham*

When Grandmama fell off the boat,
And couldn't swim (and wouldn't float),
Matilda just stood by and smiled.
I almost could have slapped the child.

13. Appreciation   *Harry Graham*

Auntie, did you feel no pain
Falling from that willow tree?
Will you do it, please, again?
'Cos my friend here didn't see.

14. Father   *Harry Graham*

During dinner at the Ritz,
Father kept on having fits,
And, which made my sorrow greater,
I was left to tip the waiter.

15. L'Enfant Glacé   *Harry Graham*

When Baby's cries grew hard to bear
I popped him in the Frigidaire.
I never would have done so if
I'd known that he'd be frozen stiff.
My wife said: 'George, I'm so unhappé!
Our darling's now completely *frappé*!

16. Tragedy   *Harry Graham*

That morning, when my wife eloped
With James, our chauffeur, how I moped!
What tragedies in life there are!
I'm dashed if I can start the car!

17. TO MY MOTHER   *George Barker*

Most near, most dear, most loved and most far,
Under the window where I often found her
Sitting as huge as Asia, seismic with laughter,
Gin and chicken helpless in her Irish hand,
Irresistible as Rabelais, but most tender for
The lame dogs and hurt birds that surround her, –
She is a procession no one can follow after
But be like a little dog following a brass band.

She will not glance up at the bomber, or condescend
To drop her gin and scuttle to a cellar,
But lean on the mahogany table like a mountain
Whom only faith can move, and so I send
O all my faith, and all my love to tell her
That she will move from mourning into morning.

18. MOTHER OF THE GROOM   *Seamus Heaney*

What she remembers
Is his glistening back
In the bath, his small boots
In the ring of boots at her feet.

Hands in her voided lap
She hears a daughter welcomed.
It's as if he kicked when lifted
And slipped her soapy hold.

Once soap would ease off
The wedding ring
That's bedded forever now
In her clapping hand.

Seamus Heaney

19. DIGGING

Between my finger and my thumb
The squat pen rests; snug as a gun.

Under my window, a clean rasping sound
When the spade sinks into gravelly ground:
My father, digging. I look down

Till his straining rump among the flowerbeds
Bends low, comes up twenty years away
Stooping in rhythm through potato drills
Where he was digging.

The coarse boot nestled on the lug, the shaft
Against the inside knee was levered firmly.
He rooted out tall tops, buried the bright edge deep
To scatter new potatoes that we picked
Loving their cool hardness in our hands.

By God, the old man could handle a spade.
Just like his old man.

My grandfather cut more turf in a day
Than any other man on Toner's bog.
Once I carried him milk in a bottle
Corked sloppily with paper. He straightened up
To drink it, then fell to right away

Nicking and slicing neatly, heaving sods
Over his shoulder, going down and down
For the good turf. Digging.

The cold smell of potato mould, the squelch and slap
Of soggy peat, the curt cuts of an edge
Through living roots awaken in my head.
But I've no spade to follow men like them.

Between my finger and my thumb
The squat pen rests.
I'll dig with it.

20. THE CAGE   *John Montague*

My father, the least happy
man I have known. His face
retained the pallor
of those who work underground:
the lost years in Brooklyn
listening to a subway
shudder the earth.

But a traditional Irishman
who (released from his grille
in the Clark Street I.R.T.)
drank neat whiskey until
he reached the only element
he felt at home in
any longer: brute oblivion.

And yet picked himself
up, most mornings,
to march down the street
extending his smile
to all sides of the good
(non negro) neighbourhood
belled by St Teresa's church.

When he came back
we walked together
across fields of Garvaghey
to see hawthorn on the summer
hedges, as though
he had never left;
a bend of the road

which still sheltered
primroses. But we
did not smile in
the shared complicity
of a dream, for when
weary Odysseus returns
Telemachus must leave.

Often as I descend
into subway or underground
I see his bald head behind
the bars of the small booth;
the mark of an old car
accident beating on his
ghostly forehead.

SECTION C
DECISIONS AND CHOICES

21. TICH MILLER *Wendy Cope*

Tich Miller wore glasses
with elastoplast-pink frames
and had one foot three sizes larger than the other.

When they picked teams for outdoor games
she and I were always the last two
left standing by the wire-mesh fence.

We avoided one another's eyes,
stooping, perhaps, to re-tie a shoelace,
or affecting interest in the flight

of some fortunate bird, and pretended
not to hear the urgent conference:
'Have Tubby!' 'No, no, have Tich!'

Usually they chose me, the lesser dud,
and she lolloped, unselected,
to the back of the other team.

At eleven we went to different schools.
In time I learned to get my own back,
sneering at hockey-players who couldn't spell.

Tich died when she was twelve.

22. Truth *Barrie Wade*

Sticks and stones may break my bones,
but words can also hurt me.
Stones and sticks break only skin,
while words are ghosts that haunt me.

Slant and curved the word-swords fall
to pierce and stick inside me.
Bats and bricks may ache through bones,
but words can mortify me.

Pain from words has left its scar
on mind and heart that's tender.
Cuts and bruises now have healed;
it's words that I remember.

Mick Gowar

23. Hero

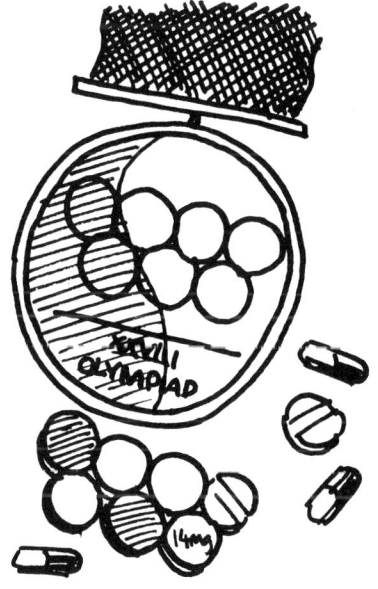

'Of course I took the drugs. Look, son,
there's no fair play, no gentlemen,
no amateurs, just winning.
How old are you? Fifteen? Well,
you should know that
no one runs for fun – well, not beyond
the schoolboy stuff, eleven or twelve years old.
I'd been a pro for years;
my job – to get that Gold.

Mind you, we English are an odd lot;
like to believe we love the slob that fails,
the gentlemanly third; so
any gap-toothed yob who gets the glory
also gets some gentlemanly trait:
helps cripples get across
the street, nice to small animals.

You know the kind of thing,
it helps the public feel it's
all legit; that sportsmanship is real and that
it's all clean fun –
the strongest, bravest, fittest
best man won.

Yeah, Steroids . . . Who do *you* think? . . . . Oh, don't be wet –
My coach, of course, he used to get them
through this vet . . . The side effects? Well, not so bad
as these things go – for eighteen months or so
I didn't have much use for girls. But, by then I was training
for the Big One – got to keep the body pure,
not waste an ounce of effort.'

He gives a great guffaw.
A chain of spittle
rattles down the front of
his pyjama jacket.
He wipes his mouth;
His eyes don't laugh at all.

'. . . Do it again? Of course I would –
I'd cheat, I'd box, I'd spike, I'd pay the devil's price
to be that good again
for just one day. You see, at twenty-three
I peaked – got all I ever wanted:
all anyone would ever want from me.
After the race, this interviewer told me
Fifty million people's hopes and dreams had been
fulfilled – a Gold!
How many ever get that chance? I did.
Would you say No to that?
Of course not.

Damn! The bell. You'd better go, they're pretty strict.
Yeah, leave the flowers there on the top,
the nurse'll get some water and a vase.'

24. LIMBO   D.M. *Thomas*

The air-gauge clamped our heartbeats. When we searched
the cabin – firm again, relentless – a
stir of limbs confirmed the needle's lurch.
How full of charm proved our young stowaway!

How to tell someone that his offence is mortal
merely in that the fuel his weight would cost, the air
he breathes, is more than one frail cosmic-ship can spare?
His grin said, *Company!* could not believe the portal

that leads to new worlds from this fetid womb
must suck him forth to – limbo. Yet he went
quietly into the airlock. There's no room
for sentiment in space. We meant

him well enough . . . Zoë, it's not our fault; you must
eat. We bear supplies for the living, put them first.

Julie O'Callaghan

25. EDIBLE ANECDOTE NO 24

the first thing you say is
'May I help you Ma'am?'
if she answers 'I'm still deciding'
well then you reply
'Our special for the day
is imported chocolate-covered cherries,
one dollar and ten cents a pound.
Would you care for a sample?'
She'll always say yes to that
even if she knows all she wants
is a pound and a half of chocolate raisins

don't watch them while they're sampling
except out of the corner of your eye
it makes them self-conscious
'My that *was* tasty' she'll sigh
as she wipes the syrup off her chin
'How much did you say those were?'
'One dollar and ten cents, Ma'am,
will I give you a pound or two?'
'Well, I *am* trying to watch my waistline,
but I will take a pound and a half
of chocolate raisins.'

then you say 'Why Ma'am, you certainly
don't look like you need to count your calories.'
as you're shovelling the raisins onto the scale
make sure she's looking and put a little extra in
that way when you say 'Will that be all?'
she may just giggle 'Oh, I'm in a naughty mood today,
you can give me a pound of those cherries as well'
say 'Yes Ma'am' humbly so she won't notice
you persuaded her.

26. THE CHOOSING *Liz Lochhead*

We were first equal Mary and I
with same coloured ribbons in mouse-coloured hair

and with equal shyness,
we curtseyed to the lady councillor
for copies of Collins' Children's Classics.
First equal, equally proud:

Best friends too Mary and I
a common bond in being cleverest (equal)
in our small school's small class.
I remember
the competition for top desk
at school service.
And my terrible fear
of her superiority at sums.

I remember the housing scheme
where we both stayed.
The same houses, different homes,
where the choices were made.

I don't know exactly why they moved,
but anyway they went.
Something about a three-room apartment
and a cheaper rent.

But from the top deck of the high-school bus
I'd glimpse among the others on the corner
Mary's father, mufflered, contrasting strangely
with the elegant greyhounds by his side.
He didn't believe in high school education,
especially for girls,
or in forking out for uniforms.

Ten years later on a Saturday –
I am coming from the library –
sitting near me on the bus,
Mary
with a husband who is tall,
curly haired, has eyes
for no one else but Mary.
Her arms are round the full-shaped vase

that is her body.
Oh, you can see where the attraction lies
in Mary's life –
not that I envy her, really.

And I am coming from the library
with my arms full of books.
I think of those prizes that were ours for the taking
and wonder when the choices got made
we don't remember making.

In this sonnet, John Magee, a 19-year-old American fighter pilot, describes some of his feelings about flying. This poem was written on the back of a letter to his parents. Not long after this he was killed on active service.

John Magee **27. HIGH FLIGHT**

Oh, I have slipped the surly bonds of earth
    And danced the skies on laughter-silvered wings;
Sunward I've climbed and joined the tumbling mirth
    Of sun-split clouds – and done a hundred things
You have not dreamed of – wheeled and soared and swung
    High in the sunlit silence. Hov'ring there
I've chased the shouting wind along and flung
    My eager craft through footless halls of air.
Up, up the long delirious burning blue
    I've topped the windswept heights with easy grace
Where never lark, or even eagle flew.
    And, while with silent, lifting mind I've trod
The high untrespassed sanctity of space,
    Put out my hand, and touched the face of God.

28. The Road Not Taken   *Robert Frost*

Two roads diverged in a yellow wood,
And sorry I could not travel both
And be one traveller, long I stood
And looked down one as far as I could
To where it bent in the undergrowth;

Then took the other, as just as fair,
And having perhaps the better claim,
Because it was grassy and wanted wear;
Though as for that the passing there
Had worn them really about the same.

And both that morning equally lay
In leaves no step had trodden black.
Oh, I kept the first for another day!
Yet knowing how way leads on to way,
I doubted if I should ever come back.

I shall be telling this with a sigh
Somewhere ages and ages hence:
Two roads diverged in a wood, and I –
I took the one less travelled by,
And that has made all the difference.

SECTION D
THE WORLD AROUND US... AND BEYOND...

29. I Wandered Lonely As a Cloud — *William Wordsworth*

I wandered lonely as a cloud
That floats on high o'er vales and hills,
When all at once I saw a crowd,
A host, of golden daffodils;
Beside the lake, beneath the trees,
Fluttering and dancing in the breeze.

Continuous as the stars that shine
And twinkle on the Milky Way,
They stretched in never-ending line
Along the margin of a bay:
Ten thousand saw I at a glance,
Tossing their heads in sprightly dance.

The waves beside them danced; but they
Outdid the sparkling waves in glee:
A poet could not but be gay,
In such a jocund company:
I gazed – and gazed – but little thought
What wealth the show to me had brought:

For oft, when on my couch I lie
In vacant or in pensive mood,
They flash upon that inward eye
Which is the bliss of solitude;
And then my heart with pleasure fills,
And dances with the daffodils.

Gerard Manley Hopkins

30. PIED BEAUTY

Glory be to God for dappled things –
    For skies of couple-colour as a brinded cow;
        For rose-moles all in stipple upon trout that swim;
Fresh-firecoal chestnut-falls; finches' wings;
    Landscape plotted and pieced – fold, fallow, and plough;
        And all trades, their gear and tackle and trim.

All things counter, original, spare, strange;
    Whatever is fickle, freckled (who knows how?)
        With swift, slow; sweet, sour; adazzle, dim;
He fathers-forth whose beauty is past change:
    Praise Him.

31. PARROT

Alan Brownjohn

Sometimes I sit with both eyes closed.
But all the same, I've heard!
They're saying. 'He won't talk because
He is a *thinking* bird.'

I'm olive-green and sulky, and
The family say, 'Oh yes,
He's silent, but he's *listening*,
He *thinks* more than he *says*!'

'He ponders on the things he hears,
Preferring not to chatter.'
 – And this is true, but *why* it's true
Is quite another matter.

I'm working out some shocking things
In order to surprise them,
And when my thoughts are ready I'll
Certainly *not* disguise them!

I'll wait, and see, and choose a time
When everyone is present.
And clear my throat and raise my beak
And give a squawk and start to speak
And go on for about a week
And it will not be pleasant!

32. Pigeons

Richard Kell

They paddle with staccato feet
In powder-pools of sunlight,
Small blue busybodies
Strutting like fat gentlemen
With hands clasped
Under their swallowtail coats;
And, as they stump about,
Their heads like tiny hammers
Tap at imaginary nails
In non-existent walls.
Elusive ghosts of sunshine
Slither down the green gloss
Of their necks an instant, and are gone.

Summer hangs drugged from sky to earth
In limpid fathoms of silence:
Only warm dark dimples of sound
Slide like slow bubbles
From the contented throats.

Raise a casual hand –
With one quick gust
They fountain into air.

33. THE BATTERY HEN
Pam Ayres

Oh, I am a battery hen,
On me back there's not a germ,
I never scratched a farmyard,
And I never pecked a worm,
I never had the sunshine,
To warm me feathers through,
Eggs I lay. Every day.
For the likes of you.

When you has them scrambled,
Piled up on your plate,
It's me what you should thank for that,
I never lays them late,
I always lays them reg'lar,
I always lays them right,
I never lays them brown,
I always lays them white.

But it's no life, for a battery hen,
In me box I'm sat,
A funnel stuck out from the side,
Me pellets comes down that,
I gets a squirt of water,
Every half a day,
Watchin' with me beady eye,
Me eggs, roll away.

I lays them in a funnel,
Strategically placed,
So that I don't kick 'em,
And let them go to waste,
They rolls off down the tubing,
And up the gangway quick,
Sometimes I gets to thinkin'
'That could have been a chick!'

I might have been a farmyard hen,
Scratchin' in the sun,
There might have been a crowd of chicks,
After me to run,
There might have been a cockerel fine,
To pay us his respects,
Instead of sittin' here,
Till someone comes and wrings our necks.

I see the Time and Motion clock,
Is sayin' nearly noon,
I 'spec me squirt of water,
Will come flyin' at me soon,
And then me spray of pellets,
Will nearly break me leg,
And I'll bite the wire nettin'
And lay one more bloody egg.

Seamus Heaney

34. Saint Francis and the Birds

When Francis preached love to the birds
They listened, fluttered, throttled up
Into the blue like a flock of words

Released for fun from his holy lips.
Then wheeled back, whirred about his head,
Pirouetted on brothers' capes,

Danced on the wing, for sheer joy played
And sang, like images took flight.
Which was the best poem Francis made,

His argument true, his tone light.

Spike Milligan

35. THE DOG LOVERS

So they bought you
And kept you in a
Very good home
Central heating
TV
A deep freeze
A *very* good home –
No one to take you
For that lovely long run –
But otherwise
'A *very* good home'.
They fed you Pal and Chum
But not that lovely long run,
Until, mad with energy and boredom
You escaped – and ran and ran and ran
Under a car.
Today they will cry for you –
Tomorrow they will buy another dog.

36. Dog Exercising Man

Keith Bosley

From the way
    they look at
        each other
it is clear
    that the man
        and the dog
are friends but
    in this park
        this morning
man does not
    exercise
        dog. On the
contrary:
    in tracksuit
        and plimsolls
the man is
    jogging eggs
        and bacon
away round
    the railings
        while the dog
is trotting
    doggedly
        as it must
along a
    concentric
        shorter track
within ear-
    shot doubtless
        wondering
what there is
    to be fetched
        and hoping
that man will
    soon mark his
        territory.

Brendan Kennelly

37. TIME FOR THE KNIFE

'You've a good one there,' Enright said.
Morrissey asked, 'Is he right for cutting yet?'
Enright lifted the terrier pup in his fist,
Slid the skin back on the gums
And fingered the neat fangs.

Caressing the brown and white head,
He handled the terrier's tail.

'Time for the knife,' he said.

The penknife from his waistcoat pocket
Flicked open. Twenty years of cutting tobacco
Had merely dented the blade.

'Let you hold the head.'
Morrissey gripped the skin behind the ears.

After he'd sharpened the knife on a stone
Enright stretched the tail
And started to cut.

It was over soon. Enright looked
At the severed tail in his fist
And pitched it into the grass.

The terrier pup
Howled as it fled,
Pursued by drops of its own blood
Regular as a pulse of pain.

For a while
It whimpered and cried alone
Like a woman mourning.

When the bleeding stopped
The stubby tail stuck up
Like a blunt warning.

38. Diary of a Church Mouse   *John Betjeman*

Here among long-discarded cassocks,
Damp stools, and half-split open hassocks,
Here where the Vicar never looks
I nibble through old service books.
Lean and alone I spend my days
Behind this Church of England baize.
I share my dark forgotten room
With two oil-lamps and half a broom.
The cleaner never bothers me,
So here I eat my frugal tea.
My bread is sawdust mixed with straw;
My jam is polish for the floor.

    Christmas and Easter may be feasts
For congregations and for priests,
And so may Whitsun. All the same,
They do not fill my meagre frame.
For me the only feast at all
Is Autumn's Harvest Festival,
When I can satisfy my want
With ears of corn around the font.
I climb the eagle's brazen head
To burrow through a loaf of bread.
I scramble up the pulpit stair
And gnaw the marrows hanging there.

    It is enjoyable to taste
These items ere they go to waste,
But how annoying when one finds
That other mice with pagan minds
Come into church my food to share
Who have no proper business there.
Two field mice who have no desire
To be baptised, invade the choir.
A large and most unfriendly rat
Comes in to see what we are at.
He says he thinks there is no God
And yet he comes . . . it's rather odd.

This year he stole a sheaf of wheat
(It screened our special preacher's seat),
And prosperous mice from fields away
Came in to hear the organ play,
And under cover of its notes
Ate through the altar's sheaf of oats.
A Low Church mouse, who thinks that I
Am too papistical, and High,
Yet somehow doesn't think it wrong
To munch through Harvest Evensong,
While I, who starve the whole year through,
Must share my food with rodents who
Except at this time of the year
Not once inside the church appear.

    Within the human world I know
Such goings-on could not be so,
For human beings only do
What their religion tells them to.
They read the Bible every day
And always, night and morning, pray,
And just like me, the good church mouse,
Worship each week in God's own house.

    But all the same it's strange to me
How very full the church can be
With people I don't see at all
Except at Harvest Festival.

Ted Hughes

39. SHEEP

The sheep has stopped crying.
All morning in her wire-mesh compound
On the lawn, she has been crying
For her vanished lamb. Yesterday they came.
Then her lamb could stand, in a fashion,
And make some tiptoe cringing steps.
Now he has disappeared.
He was only half the proper size,

And his cry was wrong. It was not
A dry little hard bleat, a baby-cry
Over a flat tongue, it was human
It was a despairing human smooth Oh!
Like no lamb I ever heard. Its hindlegs
Cowered in under its lumped spine,
Its feeble hips leaned towards
Its shoulders for support. Its stubby
White wool pyramid head, on a tottery neck,
Had sad and defeated eyes, pinched, pathetic,
Too small, and it cried all the time
Oh! Oh! staggering towards
Its alert, baffled, stamping, storming mother
Who feared our intentions. He was too weak
To find her teats, or to nuzzle up in under,
He hadn't the gumption. He was fully
Occupied just standing, then shuffling

Towards where she'd removed to. She knew
He wasn't right, she couldn't
Make him out. Then his rough-curl legs,
So stoutly built, and hooved
With real quality tips,
Just got in the way, like a loose bundle
Of firewood he was cursed to manage,
Too heavy for him, lending sometimes
Some support, but no strength, no real help.
When we sat his mother on her tail, he mouthed
   her teat,
Slobbered a little, but after a minute
Lost aim and interest, his muzzle wandered,
He was managing a difficulty
Much more urgent and important. By evening
He could not stand. It was not
That he could not thrive, he was born
With everything but the will –
That can be deformed, just like a limb.
Death was more interesting to him.
Life could not get his attention.
So he died, with the yellow birth-mucus
Still in his cardigan.
He did not survive a warm summer night.
Now his mother has started crying again.
The wind is oceanic in the elms
And the blossom is all set.

40. THE FOX

Adrian Mitchell

A fox among the shadows of the town,
Should I surrender to the arms of man?
    On the blank icehills lies in wait
    The fighting cold who has thrown down
    His challenge. I'll not imitate
    The feline compromise. I scan
    With warring eyes the servile fate
Of animals who joined the heated town.

Lean-hearted lions in the concrete zoo
Grow bellies, tendons slacken in pale hide,
    Their breath slows to a dying pace.
    Their keepers love them? Tell me who
    Would cage his love in such a place,
    Where only fish are satisfied?
    The keeper has a huntsman's face.
His grasping love would kill me in the zoo.

A scavenger throughout the snowing wind
I peel the sweet bark from the frozen tree
    Or trap the bird with springing jaws.
    The sun retreats out of my mind.
    How could I give this waking pause
    When death's my sleeping company?
    Mad empty, licking at my sores,
I howl this bitter and unloving wind.

Furious in the savage winter day
The crimson riders hounded me from birth
    Through landscapes built of thorn and stone.
    Though I must be their sudden prey,
    Torn to my terror's skeleton,
    Or go to the forgotten earth;
    I will have hunted too, alone,
I will have wandered in my handsome day.

Four seasons wrestle me, I throw them all
And live to tumble with another year
    In love or battle. I'll not fly
    From mindless elements and fall
    A victim to the keeper's lie.
    The field is mine; but still I fear
    Strong death, my watching enemy,
Though seasons pass and I survive them all.

41. THE TYGER

William Blake

Tyger! Tyger! burning bright
In the forests of the night,
What immortal hand or eye
Could frame thy fearful symmetry?

In what distant deeps or skies
Burnt the fire of thine eyes?
On what wings dare he aspire?
What the hand dare seize the fire?

And what shoulder, and what art,
Could twist the sinews of thy heart?
And when thy heart began to beat,
What dread hand? And what dread feet?

What the hammer? What the chain?
In what furnace was thy brain?
What the anvil? What dread grasp
Dare its deadly terrors clasp?

When the stars threw down their spears,
And water'd heaven with their tears,
Did He smile His work to see?
Did He who made the Lamb make thee?

Tyger! Tyger! burning bright
In the forests of the night,
What immortal hand or eye,
Dare frame thy fearful symmetry?

42. Fog *Carl Sandburg*

The fog comes
on little cat feet.

It sits looking
over harbour and city
on silent haunches
and then moves on.

43. Rogue Leaf

Derek Mahon

Believe it or not
I hung on all winter
outfacing wind and snow.

Now that spring
comes and the birds sing
I am letting go.

44. March

Patrick Kavanagh

The trees were in suspense,
Listening with an intense
Anxiety for the Word
That in the Beginning stirred
The dark-branched Tree
Of Humanity.

Subjectively the dogs
Hunted the muted bogs,
The horses suppressed their neighing,
No donkey-kind was braying,
The hare and rabbit under –
Stood the cause of wonder.

The blackbird of the yew
Alone broke the two
Minutes' silence
With a new poem's violence.
A tomboy scare that drove
Faint thoughts of active love.

45. Spring

Gerard Manley Hopkins

Nothing is so beautiful as spring –
   When weeds, in wheels, shoot long and lovely and lush;
   Thrush's eggs look little low heavens, and thrush
Through the echoing timber does so rinse and wring
The ear, it strikes like lightnings to hear him sing;
   The glassy pear-tree leaves and blooms, they brush
   The descending blue; that blue is all in a rush
With richness; the racing lambs too have fair their fling.

What is all this juice and all this joy?
   A strain of the earth's sweet being in the beginning
In Eden garden. Have, get, before it cloy,
   Before it cloud, Christ, Lord, and sour with sinning,
Innocent mind and Mayday in girl and boy,
   Most, O maid's child, thy choice and worthy the winning.

46. To Autumn
John Keats

Season of mists and mellow fruitfulness,
   Close bosom-friend of the maturing sun;
Conspiring with him how to load and bless
   With fruit the vines that round the thatch-eaves run;
To bend with apples the moss'd cottage-trees,
   And fill all fruit with ripeness to the core;
   To swell the gourd, and plump the hazel shell;
With a sweet kernel; to set budding more,
   And still more, later flowers for the bees,
Until they think warm days will never cease,
   For Summer has o'er-brimm'd their clammy cells.

Who hath not seen thee oft amid thy store?
   Sometimes whoever seeks abroad may find
Thee sitting careless on a granary floor,
   Thy hair soft-lifted by the winnowing wind;
Or on a half-reap'd furrow sound asleep,
   Drows'd with the fume of poppies, while thy hook
   Spares the next swath and all its twined flowers;
And sometimes like a gleaner thou dost keep
   Steady thy laden head across a brook;
   Or by a cider-press, with patient look,
   Thou watchest the last oozings, hours by hours.

Where are the songs of Spring? Ay, where are they?
    Think not of them, thou hast thy music too, –
While barred clouds bloom the soft-dying day,
    And touch the stubble-plains with rosy hue;
Then in a wailful choir the small gnats mourn
    Among the river sallows, borne aloft
    Or sinking as the light wind lives or dies;
And full-grown lambs loud bleat from hilly bourn;
    Hedge-crickets sing; and now with treble soft
    The red-breast whistles from a garden-croft;
And gathering swallows twitter in the skies.

47. WINTER   *L.A.G. Strong*

The winter trees like great sweep's brushes
Poke up from deep earth, black and bare,
Suddenly stir, and shake a crowd
Of sooty rooks into the air.

48. Stopping by Woods on a Snowy Evening *Robert Frost*

Whose woods these are I think I know.
His house is in the village though;
He will not see me stopping here
To watch his woods fill up with snow.

My little horse must think it queer
To stop without a farmhouse near
Between the wood and frozen lake
The darkest evening of the year.

He gives his harness bells a shake
To ask if there is some mistake.
The only other sound's the sweep
Of easy wind and downy flake.

The woods are lovely, dark and deep,
But I have promises to keep,
And miles to go before I sleep,
And miles to go before I sleep.

49. The Wood *Derek Mahon*

A frightened shriek in the wood,
the whining saw spins free,
and the puff of dust
lost in the mist
is the hurt spirit escaping
from the throat of the stricken tree.

50. THE SHELL *James Stephens*

And then I pressed the shell
Close to my ear
And listened well.
And straightway, like a bell,
Came low and clear
The slow, sad murmur of far distant seas
Whipped by an icy breeze
Upon a shore
Wind-swept and desolate.
It was a sunless strand that never bore
The footprint of a man,
Nor felt the weight
Since time began
Of any human quality or stir,
Save what the dreary winds and waves incur.

And in the hush of waters was the sound
Of pebbles, rolling round;
For ever rolling, with a hollow sound:
And bubbling sea-weeds as the waters go,
Swish to and fro
Their long cold tentacles of slimy grey.
There was no day;
Nor ever came a night
Setting the stars alight
To wonder at the moon:
Was twilight only, and the frightened croon,
Smitten to whimpers, of the dreary wind
And waves that journeyed blind. . . .
And then I loosed my ear – Oh, it was sweet
To hear a cart go jolting down the street.

51. THE TROUT *John Montague*

Flat on the bank I parted
Rushes to ease my hands
In the water without a ripple
And tilt them slowly downstream
To where he lay, tendril light
In his fluid sensual dream.

Bodiless lord of creation
I hung briefly above him
Savouring my own absence
Senses expanding in the slow
Motion, the photographic calm
That grows before action.

As the curve of my hands
Swung under his body
He surged, with visible pleasure.
I was so preternaturally close
I could count every stipple
But still cast no shadow, until

The two palms crossed in a cage
Under the lightly pulsing gills.
Then (entering my own enlarged
Shape, which rode on the water)
I gripped. To this day I can
Taste his terror on my hands.

52. The Song of the Whale *Kit Wright*

Heaving mountain in the sea,
Whale, I heard you
Grieving.

Great whale, crying for your life,
Crying for your kind, I knew
How we would use
Your dying:

Lipstick for our painted faces,
Polish for our shoes.

Tumbling mountain in the sea
Whale, I heard you
Calling.

Bird-high notes, keening, soaring:
At their edge a tiny drum
Like a heartbeat.

We would make you
Dumb.

In the forest of the sea,
Whale, I heard you
Singing,

Singing to your kind.
We'll never let you be.
Instead of life we choose

Lipstick for our painted faces
Polish for our shoes.

53. The River God
Stevie Smith

I may be smelly and I may be old,
Rough in my pebbles, reedy in my pools,
But where my fish float by I bless their swimming
And I like the people to bathe in me, especially women.
But I can drown the fools
Who bathe too close to the weir, contrary to rules.
And they take a long time drowning
As I throw them up now and then in a spirit of clowning.
Hi yih, yippity-yap, merrily I flow,
O I may be an old foul river but I have plenty of go.
Once there was a lady who was too bold
She bathed in me by the tall black cliff where the water runs cold,
So I brought her down here
To be my beautiful dear.
Oh will she stay with me will she stay
This beautiful lady, or will she go away?
She lies in my beautiful deep river bed with many a weed
To hold her, and many a waving reed.
Oh who would guess what a beautiful white face lies there
Waiting for me to smooth and wash away the fear
She looks at me with. Hi yih, do not let her
Go. There is no one on earth who does not forget her
Now. They say I am a foolish smelly river
But they do not know of my wide original bed
Where the lady waits, with her golden sleepy head.
If she wishes to go I will not forgive her.

Seamus Heaney

54. The Diviner

Cut from the green hedge a forked hazel stick
That he held tight by the arms of the V:
Circling the terrain, hunting the pluck
Of water, nervous, but professionally

Unfussed. The pluck came sharp as a sting.
The rod jerked down with precise convulsions,
Spring water suddenly broadcasting
Through a green aerial its secret stations.

The bystanders would ask to have a try.
He handed them the rod without a word.
It lay dead in their grasp till nonchalantly
He gripped expectant wrists. The hazel stirred.

John Montague

55. Like Dolmens Round my Childhood, the Old People

Like dolmens round my childhood, the old people.

Jamie MacCrystal sang to himself,
A broken song without tune, without words;
He tipped me a penny every pension day,
Fed kindly crusts to winter birds.
When he died, his cottage was robbed,
Mattress and money-box torn and searched.
Only the corpse they didn't disturb.

Maggie Owens was surrounded by animals,
A mongrel bitch and shivering pups,
Even in her bedroom a she-goat cried.
She was a well of gossip defiled,
Fanged chronicler of a whole countryside;
Reputed a witch, all I could find
Was her lonely need to deride.

The Nialls lived along a mountain lane
Where heather bells bloomed, clumps of foxglove.
All were blind, with Blind Pension and Wireless,
Dead eyes serpent-flicked as one entered
To shelter from a downpour of mountain rain.
Crickets chirped under the rocking hearthstone
Until the muddy sun shone out again.

Mary Moore lived in a crumbling gatehouse,
Famous as Pisa for its leaning gable.
Bag-apron and boots, she tramped the fields
Driving lean cattle from a miry stable.
A by-word for fierceness, she fell asleep
Over love stories, *Red Star* and *Red Circle*,
Dreamed of gypsy love rites, by firelight sealed.

Wild Billy Eagleson married a Catholic servant girl
When all his Loyal family passed on:
We danced round him shouting 'To Hell with King Billy',
And dodged from the arc of his flailing blackthorn.
Forsaken by both creeds, he showed little concern
Until the Orange drums banged past in the summer
And bowler and sash aggressively shone.

Curate and doctor trudged to attend them,
Through knee-deep snow, through summer heat,
From main road to lane to broken path,
Gulping the mountain air with painful breath.
Sometimes they were found by neighbours,
Silent keepers of a smokeless hearth,
Suddenly cast in a mould of death.

Ancient Ireland, indeed! I was reared by her bedside,
The rune and the chant, evil eye and averted head,
Fomorian fierceness of family and local feud.
Gaunt figures of fear and of friendliness,
For years they trespassed on my dreams,
Until once, in a standing circle of stones,
I felt their shadows pass

Into that dark permanence of ancient forms.

William Stafford

56. AT THE BOMB TESTING SITE

At noon in the desert a panting lizard
waited for history, its elbows tense,
watching the curve of a particular road
as if something might happen.

It was looking at something farther off
than people could see, an important scene
acted in stone for little selves
at the flute end of consequences.

There was just a continent without much on it
under a sky that never cared less.
Ready for a change, the elbows waited,
the hands gripped hard on the desert.

William Wordsworth

57. The World is Too Much With Us

The world is too much with us; late and soon,
Getting and spending, we lay waste our powers:
Little we see in Nature that is ours;
We have given our hearts away, a sordid boon!
This Sea that bares her bosom to the moon;
The winds that will be howling at all hours,
And are up-gathered now like sleeping flowers;
For this, for everything, we are out of tune;
It moves us not. – Great God! I'd rather be
A Pagan suckled in a creed outworn;
So might I, standing on this pleasant lea,
Have glimpses that would make me less forlorn;
Have sight of Proteus rising from the sea;
Or hear old Triton blow his wreathéd horn.

AND BEYOND . . .

58. SPACE SHOT
Gareth Owen

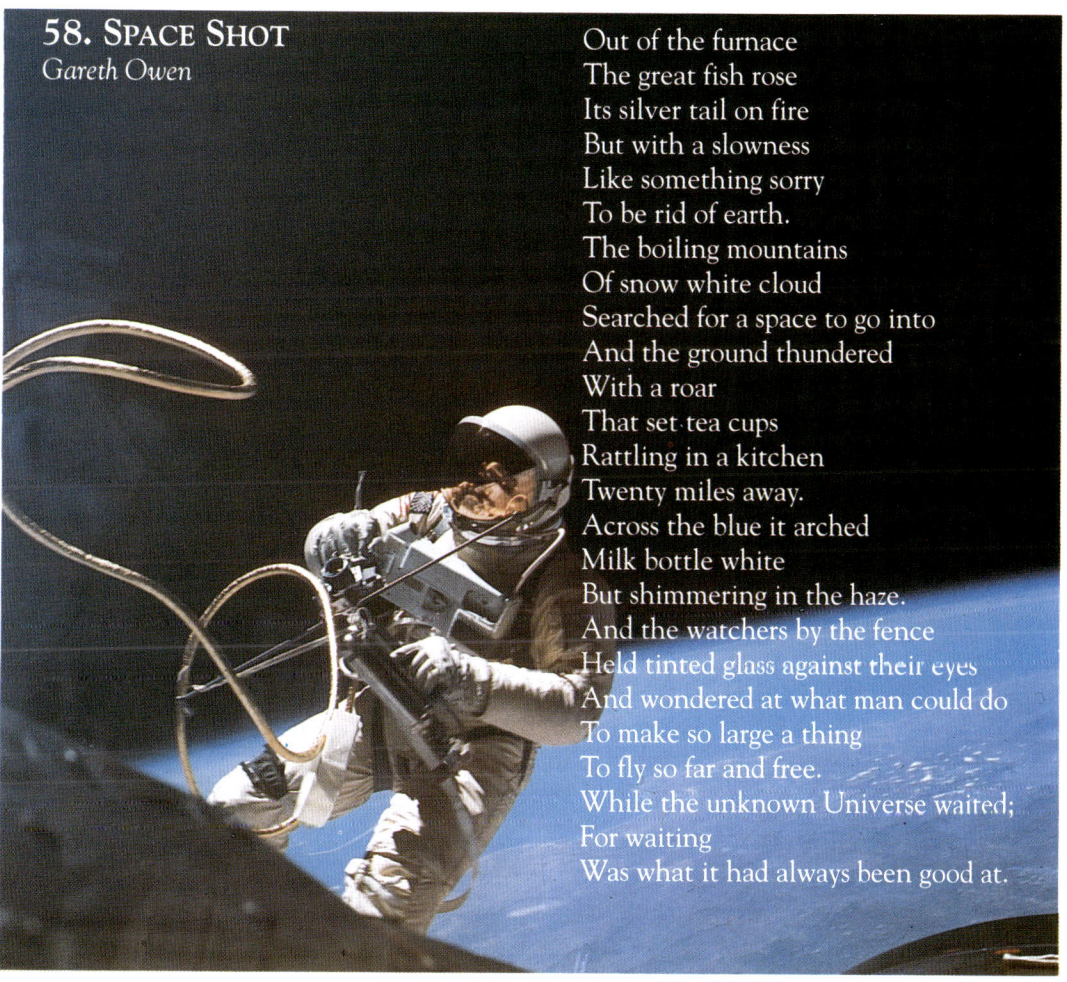

Out of the furnace
The great fish rose
Its silver tail on fire
But with a slowness
Like something sorry
To be rid of earth.
The boiling mountains
Of snow white cloud
Searched for a space to go into
And the ground thundered
With a roar
That set tea cups
Rattling in a kitchen
Twenty miles away.
Across the blue it arched
Milk bottle white
But shimmering in the haze.
And the watchers by the fence
Held tinted glass against their eyes
And wondered at what man could do
To make so large a thing
To fly so far and free.
While the unknown Universe waited;
For waiting
Was what it had always been good at.

59. THE SWIRLING WORLD STANDS STILL *John Kitching*

The swirling world stands still
As I speed on and on
Through aching space
Of stars and light from yesterday.

I cannot tell you why
I make this search. I only know
The ever-hungry asking
Of the human race.

60. RETIRED *Iain Crichton Smith*

He was tired after his voyages,
the shuttles from planet to planet
from star to star.

In the late evening
he would sway in his rocking chair
and watch the moon through the trees.

'I was there once,' he thought
'I stood on that globe.
Now it is like a football
shining in space.'

And he could hardly believe it
that in his helmet
and in his bulky space suit
he'd stirred that far dust.

61. ASTRONAUT *Derek Mahon*

Give me some information
on China and Greece;
the only place
I ever went was the moon.

62. THE BEAUTIFUL STRANGERS   *James Kirkup*

(*after sighting an Unidentified Flying Object*)

They are above us,
Beyond us and around us,
Out of space out of time.

Between star and star,
New moons, and beings wiser
Than ourselves, approach.

Our earth is rotten
As fruit about to drop
Into nothingness.

They are gardeners
Of space, who come to tend us.
Strangers, they love us.

Strangers, they love us.

In ages long past
They came to our planet.
We drove them away.

Ever since that day
Our world moves to destruction.
Death grows among us.

Only if we call
To the beautiful strangers
Will our peace return.

I know they watch me
As I write this poem now.
Poets are cosmic.

I feel their silence
Like words, their absence like love.
I belong not to this earth.

I belong to them, and they
Are my brothers, their space my home
That is not of this earth.

Ever a stranger, I came
From further fields, an outer place
Whose clouds I trail to death.

Ever a white shadow wandering
On this lost world, white and alone
Among the crowding shades of black,

My one voice cries to you, men
Of earth, out of my solitude,
That we must turn to them.

We must watch for them.
We must give our hearts and souls,
Open eyes and arms.

Look to the heavens
And upon the ground for signs.
They are among us as I am among you.

And we shall see them
With the eyes of vision, if
We have sense to see.

And we shall know them
By their purity and grace,
If we have hearts to feel.

Where are my lost brothers?
Let them come back to me!
Let us return to them!

They are above us,
Beyond us and around us,
Out of space out of time.

63. E. T. *Jean Kenward*

'Extra Terrestrial' they called you,
　spilling
suddenly from your chariot of light,
dark
in a darkling country.
Through the bracken
your fingers fumbled.
You were never quite
with us,
but only nearly –
seemed a stranger,
yet eager to be friendly,
not to fight.

Will it be possible some day to venture
ourselves into your planet?
Leave behind
the guns, the tanks, the hatred –
carry merely
the mild, inquiring searchlights
of the mind?
Not wishing to possess
your place,
but really
prove to be simply curious,
and kind?

SECTION E
LOVE

64. KING OF THE KURZEL

Mick Gowar

The Kurzel, Southend:
biggest loudest most
beautiful and brightest
gorgeous pleasure dome a
huge exploding crimson
blur electric blue a
whirling golden gleaming
jewel
sat by a sludge brown sea
All teeming human life left
miles and miles beneath:
   the biggest
everything in all the world

The photograph is
black and white
it shows
two people
of about fourteen
in pale grey uniforms
one boy, one girl
The boy at first sight
seems to have a broken arm
around the girl
his hand a

curious limp epaulette
at her shoulder
his hand seems
scared, the intimacy
too much, too soon
   they grin:
the girl has
both eyes lightly closed

the boy is me
the day was
it
the day of days
the outing of
the ATC and GVC
All month I'd prayed:
Oh, let her see me
don't let her see my nose, but
let her see me

I sat behind her
on the coach trip going down
appeared by chance
beside her
on the dipper
My dreams came true
She clutched my hand, clung,
held it harder when
the ride was over
kept on holding . . .

On the waltzer –
snaked my arm around her shoulders
She didn't shake it off
When we got off
hers wound itself
around my waist

(I couldn't breathe, believe it
never wanted such a joy
to end)

In the throng, that thrill
that thump, thump in my throat
So loud I'm sure she heard
my heart pound Oh, I love you

She kissed me on the coach
 – not once, but over and over and over
And all the spinning, swirling
bucking bronco rides

were nothing, nothing like that
The coloured lights, the crowds
had witnessed
the great moment –
Me, grown-up
She'd shown them all
her lovely arms
around me
like a crown

65. Girl's Song   *Wilfrid Gibson*

I was so happy that I hardly knew it
Nor ever guessed that life was not all play,
And little dreamt I'd live to see the dawning
Of such a day –
Oh, why, why should it be
That suddenly
Life should seem strange and terrible to me?

I'd never cared for lads like other lasses
Nor heeded overmuch what they might say,
And little dreamt I'd live to see the dawning
Of such a day –
Oh, why, why should it be
That suddenly
A lad's word should mean life and death to me?

66. HE WISHES FOR THE CLOTHS OF HEAVEN   W.B. Yeats

Had I the heavens' embroidered cloths,
Enwrought with golden and silver light,
The blue and the dim and the dark cloths
Of night and light and the half-light,
I would spread the cloths under your feet:
But I, being poor, have only my dreams;
I have spread my dreams under your feet;
Tread softly because you tread on my dreams.

Adam Pritchard

67. FIRST KISS

Suddenly;
(after nearly an hour of fidgeting about
on the cold manky steps of her flats
– and she really did have to go in you know –)

our cracked lips rustled
and I had my first taste of her chewing-gum-mouth.

Adrian Henri

68. SONG FOR A BEAUTIFUL GIRL PETROL-PUMP ATTENDANT ON THE MOTORWAY

I wanted your soft verges
But you gave me the hard shoulder.

69. The Passionate Shepherd to His Love

Christopher Marlowe

Come live with me and be my love,
And we will all the pleasures prove,
That hills and valleys, dales and fields,
And all the craggy mountains yields.

There we will sit upon the rocks,
And see the shepherds feed their flocks,
By shallow rivers to whose falls
Melodious birds sing madrigals.

And I will make thee beds of roses
With a thousand fragrant posies,
A cap of flowers, and a kirtle
Embroidered all with leaves of myrtle;

A gown made of the finest wool
Which from our pretty lambs we pull;
Fair lined slippers for the cold,
With buckles of the purest gold;

A belt of straw and ivy buds,
With coral clasps and amber studs:
And if these pleasures may thee move,
Come live with me and be my love.

The shepherd swains shall dance and sing
For thy delight each May morning:
If these delights thy mind may move,
Then live with me and be my love.

70. The Passionate Astronaut to His Love

Greg Smenda

Come live with me, and be my mate
And we'll enjoy a pleasure spate,
Of hills, rocks, dales and lunar sand
And all the craggy mountains grand.

There we will sit on lunar crust
Seeing the robot tractor's thrust
By shallow craters to whose walls
Engines hum electronic madrigals.

And I will make you beds of plastic
With many controls that are fantastic
A helmet of most mod design
Printed silver with I.D. sign.

A space suit made of finest nylon
Made in labs to keep its style on
Synthetic lined boots for the freeze
With zips that shut and open with ease.

A utility belt and antenna buds
With metal clasps and platinum studs
And if these things will make your scene
Come live with me – we'll make a team.

The astronaut colony shall for you sing
The earphones filled with zong and zing.
So if these things do switch you on
Come live with me, – my mate, come on!

Liz Loxley   **71. The Thickness of Ice**

At first we will meet as friends
(Though secretly I'll be hoping
We'll become much more
And hoping that you're hoping that too).

At first we'll be like skaters
Testing the thickness of ice
(With each meeting
We'll skate nearer the centre of the lake).

Later we will become less anxious to impress,
Less eager than the skater going for gold,
(The triple jumps and spins
Will become an old routine:
We will be content with simple movements).

Later we will not notice the steady thaw,
The creeping cracks will be ignored,
(And one day when the ice gives way
We will scramble to save ourselves
And not each other).

Last of all we'll meet as acquaintances
(Though secretly we will be enemies,
Hurt by missing out on a medal,
Jealous of new partners).

Last of all we'll be like children
Having learnt the thinness of ice,
(Though secretly, perhaps, we may be hoping
To break the ice between us
And maybe meet again as friends).

72. Lady Diamond   *Unknown*

There was a king, and a glorious king,
    A king of noble fame,
And he had daughters only one,
    Lady Diamond was her name.

He had a boy, a kitchen boy,
    A boy of muckle scorn,
She loved him long, she loved him aye,
    Till the grass o'er grew the corn.

When twenty weeks were gone and past,
    O she began to greet,
For her petticoats grew short before,
    And her stays they wouldn't meet.

It fell upon one winter's night,
    The king could get no rest,
He came unto his daughter dear,
    Just like a wandering ghost.

He came unto her bed chamber,
    Pulled back the curtains long,
'What aileth thee my daughter dear,
    I fear you have gotten wrong.'

'O if I have, despise me not,
    For he is all my joy,
I will forsake both dukes and earls
    And marry your kitchen boy.'

'O bring to me my merry men all,
    By thirty and by three,
O bring me my kitchen boy,
    We'll murder him secretly.'

There was not a sound into the hall,
    And ne'er a word was said,
Until they got him safe and sure,
    Between two feather beds.

'Cut the heart from out of his breast,
    Put it in a cup of gold,
And present it to his Diamond dear,
    For she was both stout and bold.'

'O come to me, my hinnie, my heart,
    O come to me my joy,
O come to me, my hinnie, my heart,
    My father's kitchen boy.'

She took the cup from out of their hands,
    And she set it at her bed head.
She washed it with tears that fell from her eyes,
    And next morning she was dead.

'O where were you my merry men all,
    That I gave meat and wage,
That you didn't stay my cruel hand,
    When I was in a rage?

For gone is all my heart's delight,
    O gone is all my joy,
For my dear Diamond she is dead,
    Likewise my kitchen boy.'

73. WOMAN IS *Robin Morgan*

— kicking strongly in your mother's womb, upon which she is
told, 'It must be a boy, if it's so active!'

— being tagged with a *pink* beaded bracelet thirty seconds
after you are born, and wrapped in *pink* blankets five minutes thereafter

— being labelled a tomboy when all you wanted to do was
climb that tree and look out and see a distance.

— learning to sit with your legs crossed, even when your feet
can't touch the floor yet.

— hating boys – because they're allowed to do things you want
to do but are forbidden to – and being told hating boys is a phase.

— wondering why your father gets mad now and then, but
your mother mostly sighs a lot.

— seeing grown-ups chuckle when you say you want to be an
engineer or doctor when you grow up – learning to say you
want to be a mommy or a nurse, instead.

— feeling basically comfortable in your own body, but gradually learning to hate it because you are: too short or tall, too fat or thin, thick-thighed or big-wristed, large-eared or stringy-haired, short-necked or long-armed, bowlegged, knock-kneed or pigeon-toed – *something* that *might* make boys not like you.

— wanting to kill yourself because of pimples, dandruff, or a natural tendency to sweat – and discovering that commercials about miracle products just lie.

— having your first real human talk with your mother and being told about all her old hopes and lost ambitions, and how you can't fight it, and that's just the way it is: life, sex, men, the works – and loving her and hating her for having been so beaten down.

— having your first real human talk with your father and being told about all *his* old hopes and lost ambitions, and how women really have it easier, and 'what a man really wants in a woman,' – and loving him and hating him for having been beaten down – and for beating down your mother in turn.

— coming home from work – and starting *in* to work: unpack the groceries, fix supper, wash up the dishes, rinse out some laundry etc., etc.

— feeling a need to say 'thank you' when your guy actually fixes *himself* a meal now that you're dying with the 'flu.

74. THE IDEAL HUSBAND
Harry Graham

A recent correspondence in the *Daily Mirror* proves that, according to popular opinion, fools make the best husbands. 'The bigger the fool,' as one writer briefly puts it, 'the better the husband.'

Though husbands bright and brainy
    May have their use, one knows,
Give me an honest zany
    As partner of my woes!
How blest indeed is woman's fate
Who takes a noodle as her mate!

The clever husband quarrels,
    Or grumbles at his food;
The wit's ideas of morals
    Are lamentably crude;
A partner with a feeble mind
Is neither vicious nor unkind.

'Tis commonly admitted,
    And ev'ry one allows,
That if a man's half-witted
    He makes a perfect spouse;
And more resigned, each day, I feel
To marriage with an imbecile!

When comes my time for mating,
    When Cupid shoots his bolt,
I don't mind frankly stating
    That I shall wed a dolt.
He must be dull who marries me;
But (as you say) he's bound to be!

75. WHEN YOU ARE OLD
W.B. Yeats

When you are old and grey and full of sleep,
And nodding by the fire, take down this book,
And slowly read, and dream of the soft look
Your eyes had once, and of their shadows deep;

How many loved your moments of glad grace,
And loved your beauty with love false or true,
But one man loved the pilgrim soul in you,
And loved the sorrows of your changing face;

And bending down beside the glowing bars
Murmur, a little sadly, how love fled
And paced upon the mountains overhead
And hid his face amid a crowd of stars.

76. Gardening Sunday *Brian Jones*

She brushes her hair out in the sun.
This could be a young girl – such absorption,

and the lifted forearm plumped. All day
we have moved together through roses,
    currants,
silently. Now she tucks up like a girl
on the kitchen step, gathering on her hair

the dwindling lustre of this Sunday,
while I wash hands, and make the tea for her.

The jars stand full of fruit. People spend
their fifty years going no farther.

*John Lennon
and
Paul McCartney*

77. When I'm Sixty-Four

When I get older losing my hair many years from now.
Will you still be sending me a valentine,
Birthday greetings, bottle of wine?
If I'd been out till quarter to three would you lock the door?
Will you still need me, will you still feed me,
When I'm sixty four?

I could be handy mending a fuse when your lights have gone.
You can knit a sweater by the fire-side,
Sunday mornings, go for a ride.
Doing the garden, digging the weeds. Who could ask for more?
Will you still need me, will you still feed me,
When I'm sixty four?

Send me a post-card, drop me a line stating point of view.
Indicate precisely what you mean to say,
Yours sincerely wasting away.
Give me an answer, fill in a form, mine forever more.
Will you still need me, will you still feed me,
When I'm sixty four?

78. YESTERDAY *Patricia Pogson*

It seems only yesterday
I balanced a tiny foot
on my palm
and marvelled
that anything
so perfect
could be so small.
Now I can fit my hand in
when I clean your shoes.

I can remember
when I was centred
round you
feeling your feet
strong and determined
testing the strength
of my rib cage
your hard heels
distorting my belly.

Now I wave you off
in the morning
and turn away
to continue
with my work
unhindered by your
eager face
grateful to be able
to make my own pace.
Yet tuned
to your return.

In time the distance
we put between us
will deprive me
of your grace.

Until then
each simple homely act
like rubbing this polish
into your shoes
will focus
    my imperfect love.

William Shakespeare

79. Shall I compare thee to a Summer's day?

Shall I compare thee to a Summers day?
Thou art more lovely and more temperate:
Rough windes do shake the darling buds of Maie,
And Sommers lease hath all too short a date:
Sometime too hot the eye of heaven shines,
And often is his gold complexion dimm'd,
And every faire from faire some-time declines,
By chance, or natures changing course untrim'd:
But thy eternall Sommer shall not fade,
Nor loose possession of that faire thou ow'st,
Nor shall death brag thou wandr'st in his shade,
When in eternall lines to time thou grow'st,
    So long as men can breath or eyes can see,
    So long lives this, and this gives life to thee.

Edmund Spenser

80. One Day I Wrote Her Name upon the Strand

One day I wrote her name upon the strand,
But came the waves, and washed it away:
Again I wrote it with a second hand,
But came the tide, and made my pains his prey.
Vain man, said she, that dost in vain assay
A mortal thing so to immortalise!
For I myself shall like to this decay,
And eek my name be wiped out likewise.
Not so (quoth I) let baser things devise
To die in dust, but you shall live by fame:
My verse your virtues rare shall eternise,
And in the heavens write your glorious name;
Where, whenas death shall all the world subdue,
Our love shall live, and later life renew.

SECTION F
BIRTH TO DEATH

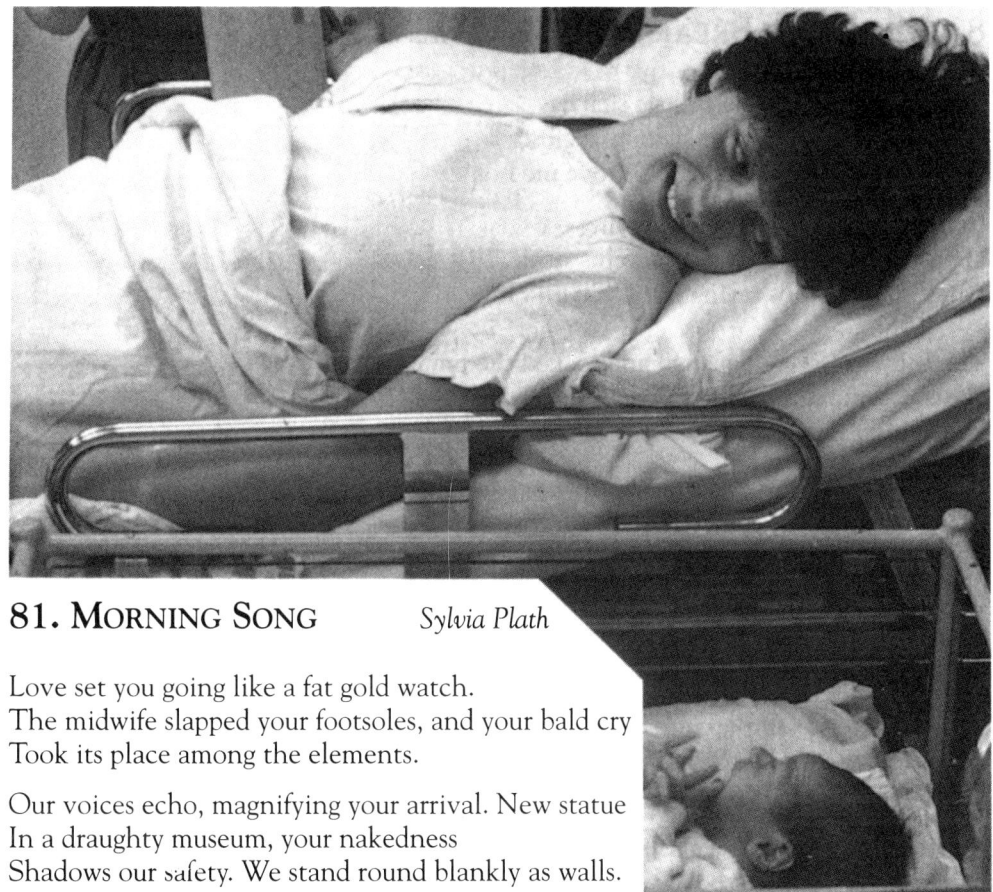

81. Morning Song   *Sylvia Plath*

Love set you going like a fat gold watch.
The midwife slapped your footsoles, and your bald cry
Took its place among the elements.

Our voices echo, magnifying your arrival. New statue
In a draughty museum, your nakedness
Shadows our safety. We stand round blankly as walls.

I'm no more your mother
Than the cloud that distils a mirror to reflect its own
Effacement at the wind's hand.

All night your moth breath
Flickers among the flat pink roses. I wake to listen:
A far sea moves in my ear.

One cry, and I stumble from bed, cow-heavy and floral
In my Victorian nightgown.
Your mouth opens clean as a cat's. The window square

Whitens and swallows its dull stars. And now you try
Your handful of notes;
The clear vowels rise like balloons.

82. The Baby

A bit of talcum
Is always walcum.

Ogden Nash

83. Mid-Term Break   *Seamus Heaney*

I sat all morning in the college sick bay
Counting bells knelling classes to a close.
At two o'clock our neighbours drove me home.

In the porch I met my father crying –
He had always taken funerals in his stride –
And Big Jim Evans saying it was a hard blow.

The baby cooed and laughed and rocked the pram
When I came in, and I was embarrassed
By old men standing up to shake my hand

And tell me they were 'sorry for my trouble',
Whispers informed strangers I was the eldest,
Away at school, as my mother held my hand

In hers and coughed out angry tearless sighs.
At ten o'clock the ambulance arrived
With the corpse, stanched and bandaged by the nurses.

Next morning I went up into the room. Snowdrops
And candles soothed the bedside; I saw him
For the first time in six weeks. Paler now,

Wearing a poppy bruise on his left temple,
He lay in the four foot box as in his cot.
No gaudy scars, the bumper knocked him clear.

A four foot box, a foot for every year.

84. The Identification   *Roger McGough*

So you think it's Stephen?
Then I'd best make sure
Be on the safe side as it were.
Ah, there's been a mistake. The hair
you see, it's black, now Stephen's fair. . . .
What's that? The explosion?
Of course, burnt black. Silly of me.
I should have known. Then let's get on.

The face, is that the face I ask?
That mask of charred wood
blistered, scarred, could
that have been a child's face?
The sweater, where intact, looks
in fact all too familiar.
But one must be sure.

The scoutbelt. Yes that's his.
I recognise the studs he hammered in
not a week ago. At the age
when boys get clothes-conscious
now you know. It's almost
certainly Stephen. But one must
be sure. Remove all trace of doubt.
Pull out every splinter of hope.

Pockets. Empty the pockets.
Handkerchief? Could be any schoolboy's.
Dirty enough. Cigarettes?
Oh this can't be Stephen.
I don't allow him to smoke you see.
He wouldn't disobey me. Not his father.

But that's his penknife. That's his
   alright.
And that's his key on the keyring
Gran gave him just the other night.
So this must be him.

I think I know what happened
. . . . . . about the cigarettes
No doubt he was minding them
for one of the older boys.
Yes that's it.
That's him.
That's our Stephen.

William Wordsworth

85. SHE DWELT AMONG THE UNTRODDEN WAYS

She dwelt among the untrodden ways
    Besides the springs of Dove,
A Maid whom there were none to praise
    And very few to love:

A Violet by a mossy stone
    Half hidden from the eye!
– Fair as a star, when only one
    Is shining in the sky.

She lived unknown, and few could know
    When Lucy ceased to be;
But she is in her grave, and oh,
    The difference to me.

86. TO WAKEN AN OLD LADY

William Carlos Williams

Old age is
a flight of small
cheeping birds
skimming
bare trees
above a snow glaze.
Gaining and failing,
they are buffeted
by a dark wind –
But what?
On harsh weedstalks
the flock has rested –
the snow
is covered with broken
seed-husks,
and the wind tempered
with a shrill
piping of plenty.

87. Good
R. S. Thomas

The old man comes out on the hill
and looks down to recall earlier days
in the valley. He sees the stream shine,
the church stand, hears the litter of
children's voices. A chill in the flesh
tells him that death is not far off
now: it is the shadow under the great boughs
of life. His garden has herbs growing.
The kestrel goes by with fresh prey
in its claws. The wind scatters the scent
of wild beans. The tractor operates
on the earth's body. His grandson is there
ploughing; his young wife fetches him
cakes and tea and a dark smile. It is well.

88. Death in the Village

Graham Hough

All afternoon she held her vague dark eyes
Bent to the window where an apple tree
Dandled its fruit and leant against the pane;
And it was through a drift of tangled leaves
That the two children she had never had
Ran home from school and whispered in the lane.

At four o'clock the husband she had not loved
Trudged round the corner, lifted up the latch
And through the slanting door let in the cold;
Turning her head she felt the chill strong breath,
And even as she waited for the kiss
Saw on his sleeve the grey churchyard mould.

And then the kettle sang, and as she stepped
Towards the kitchen threshold, there were two
Who many a year ago had courted her;
And she had not been kind; but there they were
Come back again, one brown with blazing eyes,
The other pale with seaweed in his hair.

A dear disorder stirred the ordered place
As all at once their voices filled the room
And dipped and circled in the air above her,
And chimed and sang and beat the silence back
In one accord, past all contention now,
Treble and bass, husband and child and lover.

She had not time to ask why they had come,
For all the voices seemed to speak one thought.
'We waited long,' they said. 'Now you are free
To come with us.' And as they crowded round,
Smiling and calm, they held her and were gone,
Before she even thought to make the tea.

The kettle hissed alone and soon burned dry;
The clock struck five; the fire died. It was years
Since kin or company had crossed the floor.
Only the cat picked out with mincing feet
His delicate way among the carpet flowers;
And all the rippled quiet lay smooth once more.

89. Let Me Die a Youngman's Death   *Roger McGough*

Let me die a youngman's death
not a clean and inbetween
the sheets holywater death
not a famous-last-words
peaceful out of breath death

When I'm 73
and in constant good tumour
may I be mown down at dawn
by a bright red sports car
on my way home
from an allnight party

Or when I'm 91
with silver hair
and sitting in a barber's chair
may rival gangsters
with hamfisted tommyguns burst in
and give me a short back and insides

Or when I'm 104
and banned from the Cavern
may my mistress
catching me in bed with her daughter
and fearing for her son
cut me up into little pieces
and throw away every piece but one

Let me die a youngman's death
not a free from sin tiptoe in
candle wax and waning death
not a curtains drawn by angels borne
'what a nice way to go' death

Alfred, Lord Tennyson

90. Crossing the Bar

Sunset and evening star,
  And one clear call for me.
And may there be no moaning of the bar,
  When I put out to sea,

But such a tide as moving seems asleep,
  Too full for sound and foam,
When that which drew from out the boundless deep
  Turns again home.

Twilight and evening bell,
  And after that the dark:
And may there be no sadness of farewell,
  When I embark;

For tho' from out our bourne of Time and Place
  The flood may bear me far,
I hope to see my Pilot face to face,
  When I have crost the bar.

91. Do not go gentle into that good night

Dylan Thomas

Do not go gentle into that good night,
Old age should burn and rave at close of day;
Rage, rage against the dying of the light.

Though wise men at their end know dark is right,
Because their words have forked no lightning they
Do not go gentle into that good night.

Good men, the last way by, crying how bright
Their frail deeds might have danced in a green bay,
Rage, rage against the dying of the light.

Wild men who caught and sang the sun in flight,
And learn, too late, they grieved it on its way,
Do not go gentle into that good night.

Grave men, near death, who see with blinding sight
Blind eyes could blaze like meteors and be gay,
Rage, rage against the dying of the light.

And you, my father, there on the sad height,
Curse, bless, me now with your fierce tears, I pray.
Do not go gentle into that good night.
Rage, rage against the dying of the light.

92. FOR EVERYTHING THERE IS A SEASON. . . . *Ecclesiastes 2*

For everything there is a season, and
a time for every matter under heaven:
a time to be born, and a time to die;
a time to plant, and a time to pluck
      up what is planted;
a time to kill, and a time to heal;
a time to break down, and a time to
      build up;
a time to weep, and a time to laugh;
a time to mourn, and a time to dance;
a time to cast away stones, and a
      time to gather stones together;
a time to embrace, and a time to
      refrain from embracing;
a time to seek, and a time to lose;
a time to keep, and a time to cast
      away;
a time to rend, and a time to sew;
a time to keep silence, and a time to
      speak;
a time to love, and a time to hate;
a time for war, and a time for peace.

SECTION G
WAR

93. FROM 'THE TÁIN'

Translated by Thomas Kinsella

At a ford on the Cronn river Cúchulainn came to meet them.
   'Laeg, my friend,' he said to his charioteer, 'the army is upon us.'
   The charioteer said:
      'I swear to the gods
         I'll do great deeds
      before these warriors
         driving to triumph
      at full force
         on slender steeds
      with yokes of silver
         and golden wheels
      to crush kings' heads
         my driven steeds
      will take us leaping
         to victory.'
Cúchulainn said:
      'Now friend Laeg
         set our course headlong
      into the crush
         for Macha's great triumph
      let them stray like women
         on the plain in terror
      the teams' heads set
         against Ailill and Medb
      through two armies
         like placid herds
      grinding among them
         our vengeful path.
   'I summon the waters to help me,' Cúchulainn said.
'I summon air and earth; but I summon now above all the Cronn river:
      'Let Cronn itself fall-to in the fight
      to save Murtheimne from the enemy
      until the warrior's work is done
      on the mountain-top of Ochaine.'
And the water reared up to the treetops.

Then Maine, son of Ailill and Medb, went out before all. Cúchulainn slew him in the ford and thirty horsemen of his company were overwhelmed with him.

Charles Wolfe

94. THE BURIAL OF SIR JOHN MOORE AFTER CORUNNA

Not a drum was heard, not a funeral note,
    As his corpse to the rampart we hurried;
Not a soldier discharged his farewell shot
    O'er the grave where our hero we buried.

We buried him darkly at dead of night,
    The sods with our bayonets turning,
By the struggling moonbeam's misty light
    And the lanthorn dimly burning.

No useless coffin enclosed his breast,
    Not in sheet or in shroud we wound him;
But he lay like a warrior taking his rest
    With his martial cloak around him.

Few and short were the prayers we said,
    And we spoke not a word of sorrow;
But we steadfastly gazed on the face that was dead,
    And we bitterly thought of the morrow.

We thought, as we hollowed his narrow bed
    And smoothed down his lonely pillow,
That the foe and the stranger would tread o'er his head,
    And we far away on the billow!

Lightly they'll talk of the spirit that's gone,
    And o'er his cold ashes upbraid him –
But little he'll reck, if they let him sleep on
    In the grave where a Briton has laid him.

But half of our heavy task was done
    When the clock struck the hour for retiring;
And we heard the distant and random gun
    That the foe was sullenly firing.

Slowly and sadly we laid him down,
    From the field of his fame fresh and gory;
We carved not a line, and we raised not a stone,
    But we left him alone with his glory.

95. The Soldier   *Rupert Brooke*

If I should die, think only this of me:
    That there's some corner of a foreign field
That is for ever England. There shall be
    In that rich earth a richer dust concealed;
A dust whom England bore, shaped, made aware,
    Gave, once, her flowers to love, her ways to roam
A body of England's, breathing English air,
    Washed by the rivers, blest by suns of home.

And think, this heart, all evil shed away,
    A pulse in the eternal mind, no less
        Gives somewhere back the thoughts by England given;
Her sights and sounds; dreams happy as her day;
    And laughter, learnt of friends; and gentleness;
        In hearts at peace, under an English heaven.

96. An Irish Airman Foresees His Death
W.B. Yeats

I know that I shall meet my fate
Somewhere among the clouds above;
Those that I fight I do not hate,
Those that I guard I do not love;
My country is Kiltartan Cross,
My countrymen Kiltartan's poor,
No likely end could bring them loss
Or leave them happier than before.
Nor law, nor duty bade me fight,
Nor public men, nor cheering crowds,
A lonely impulse of delight
Drove to this tumult in the clouds;
I balanced all, brought all to mind,
The years to come seemed waste of breath,
A waste of breath the years behind
In balance with this life, this death.

John McCrea
97. In Flanders Fields

In Flanders fields the poppies blow
Between the crosses, row on row
    That mark our place; and in the sky
    The larks, still bravely singing, fly
Scarce heard amid the guns below.

We are the Dead. Short days ago
We lived, felt dawn, saw sunset glow,
    Loved and were loved, and now we lie
    In Flanders fields.

Take up our quarrel with the foe:
To you from failing hands we throw
    The torch; be yours to hold it high.
    If ye break faith with us who die
We shall not sleep, though poppies grow
    In Flanders fields.

Military Manoeuvres by Richard Moynan (National Gallery of Ireland)

Wilfred Owen   **98. Dulce et Decorum est**

    Bent double, like old beggars under sacks,
    Knock-kneed, coughing like hags, we cursed through sludge,
    Till on the haunting flares we turned our backs,
    And towards our distant rest began to trudge.
    Men marched asleep. Many had lost their boots
    But limped on, blood-shod. All went lame; all blind;
    Drunk with fatigue; deaf even to the hoots
    Of tired, outstipped Five-Nines that dropped behind.

    Gas! Gas! Quick, boys! – An ecstasy of fumbling,
    Fitting the clumsy helmets just in time;
    But someone still was yelling out and stumbling,
    And flound'ring like a man in fire or lime. . . .
    Dim, through the misty panes and thick green light,
    As under a green sea, I saw him drowning.
    In all my dreams, before my helpless sight,
    He plunges at me, guttering, choking, drowning.

If in some smothering dreams, you too could pace
Behind the wagon that we flung him in,
And watch the white eyes writhing in his face,
His hanging face, like a devil's sick of sin;
If you could hear, at every jolt, the blood
Come gargling from the froth-corrupted lungs,
Obscene as cancer, bitter as the cud
Of vile, incurable sores on innocent tongues, –
My friend, you would not tell with such high zest
To children ardent for some desperate glory,
The old Lie: *Dulce et decorum est
Pro patria mori*.

99. THE GENERAL

Siegfried Sassoon

'Good-morning; good-morning!' the General said
When we met him last week on our way to the line.
Now the soldiers he smiled at are most of 'em dead,
And we're cursing his staff for incompetent swine.
'He's a cheery old card,' grunted Harry to Jack
As they slogged up to Arras with rifle and pack.

* * * * * *

But he did for them both by his plan of attack.

100. MILITARY SERVICE

Elizabeth Jennings

He will not hurt because he is afraid.
He tries to force a hate he does not feel.
He practises all night but is dismayed
When morning comes to shine upon his steel
To find he handles it as if he played

With caps and pistols, noise which never hurt.
He has a bayonet and feels the knife
With fingering pride. He has become alert
As if to kill would give him double life
But plunging steel in sawdust dulls his heart.

He has not proved his manhood, thinks of waste,
Of sweating hours when he's too bored to read.
Then anger starts that he has been so placed,
Playing the guard of other's fear and greed.
His fight is like loveless kisses, a sour taste.

Siegfried Sassoon

101. THE HERO

'Jack fell as he'd have wished,' Mother said,
And folded up the letter that she'd read.
'The Colonel writes so nicely.' Something broke
In the tired voice that quavered to a choke.
She half looked up. 'We mothers are so proud
Of our dead soldiers.' Then her face was bowed.

Quietly the Brother Officer went out.
He'd told the poor old dear some gallant lies
That she would nourish all her days, no doubt.
For while he coughed and mumbled, her weak eyes
Had shone with gentle triumph, brimmed with joy,
Because he'd been so brave, her glorious boy.

He thought how 'Jack', cold-footed, useless swine,
Had panicked down the trench that night the mine
Went up at Wicked Corner*; how he'd tried
To get sent home, and how, at last, he died,
Blown to small bits. And no one seemed to care
Except that lonely woman with white hair.

* part of a trench system

C.P.S. Denholm-Young

102. DEAD GERMAN YOUTH

He lay there, mutilated and forlorn,
Save that his face was woundless, and his hair
Drooped forward and caressed his boyish brow.
He looked so tired, as if his life had been
Too full of pain and anguish to endure,

And like a weary child who tires of play
He lay there, waiting for decay.
I feel no anger towards you, German boy,
Whom war has driven down the path of pain.
Would God we could have met in peace
And laughed and talked with tankards full of beer,
For I would rather hear your youthful mirth
At stories which I often loved to tell
Than stand here looking down at you
So terrible, so quiet and so still.

103. Killed in Action

Juliette de Bairacli-Levy

For N.J. De B.-L.
Crete, May, 1941

His chair at the table, empty,
His home clothes hanging in rows forlorn,
His cricket bat and cap, his riding cane,
The new flannel suit he had not worn.
His dogs, restless, restless, with tortured ears
Listening for his swift, light tread upon the path.
And there – his violin! Oh his violin! Hush! hold your tears.

104. Shells
Wilfrid Gibson

All day like an automaton
She fits the shells into the gauge,
Hour after hour, to earn the wage
To keep her and her little son:
All day, hour after hour, she stands
Handling cold death with calloused hands.

She dare not think, she dare not feel
What happens to the shells that she
Handles and checks so carefully,
Or what, within each case of steel
Is packed as, hour by hour she stands
Handling cold death with calloused hands.

R.S. Thomas
105. The Evacuee

She woke up under a loose quilt
Of leaf patterns, woven by the light
At the small window, busy with the boughs
Of a young cherry; but wearily she lay,
Waiting for the siren[1], slow to trust
Nature's deceptive peace, and then afraid
Of the long silence, she would have crept
Uneasily from the bedroom with its frieze[2]
Of fresh sunlight, had not a cock crowed,
Shattering the surface of that limpid[3] pool
Of stillness, and before the ripples died
One by one in the field's shallows,
The farm woke with uninhibited[4] din.

And now the noise and not the silence drew her
Down the bare stairs at great speed.
The sounds and voices were a rough sheet
Waiting to catch her, as though she leaped
From the scorched storey[5] of the charred past.

And there the table and the gallery
Of farm faces trying to be kind
Beckoned her nearer, and she sat down
Under an awning[6] of salt hams.

And so she grew, a small bird in the nest
Of welcome that was built about her,
Home now after so long away
In the flowerless streets of the drab town.
The men watched her busy with her hens,
The soft flesh ripening warm as corn
On the sticks of limbs, the grey eyes clear,
Rinsed with dew of their long dread.
The men watched her, and, nodding, smiled
With earth's charity, patient and strong.

1 air-raid warning
2 band of sunlight on a wall
3 clear
4 unrestrained
5 burning building
6 overhang

106. PIGTAIL

Tadeusz Różewicz
(Translated by
Adam Czerniawski)

When all the women in the transport
had their heads shaved
four workmen with brooms made of birch twigs
swept up
and gathered up the hair

Behind clean glass
the stiff hair lies
of those suffocated in gas chambers
there are pins and side combs
in this hair

The hair is not shot through with light
is not parted by the breeze
is not touched by any hand
or rain or lips

In huge chests
clouds of dry hair
of those suffocated
and a faded plait
a pigtail with a ribbon
pulled at school
by naughty boys.

The Museum, Auschwitz, 1948

107. Even Hitler had a mother
Herbert Farjeon

Even Hitler had a mother,
Even Mussolini had a ma,
When they were babies they said Goo, goo, goo,
And sucked their thumbs, and got wet through.
Don't be hard upon the Blackshirts,
They may be rather Swastika,
      But
Even Hitler had a mother
      And
Even Mussolini had a ma.

Roger McGough

108. Icarus Allsorts

'A meteorite is reported to have landed
in New England. No damage is said . . .'

A littlebit of heaven fell
From out of the sky one day
It landed in the ocean
Not so very far away
The General at the radar screen
Rubbed his hands with glee
And grinning pressed the button
That started World War Three

From every corner of the earth
Bombs began to fly
There were even missile jams
No traffic lights in the sky
In the time it takes to blow your nose
The people fell, the mushrooms rose

'House!' cried the fatlady
As the bingohall moved to various parts
Of the town

'Raus!' cried the German butcher
As his shop came tumbling down

Philip was in the countinghouse
Counting out his money
The Queen was in the parlour
Eating bread and honey
When through the window
Flew a bomb
And made them go all funny

In the time it takes to draw a breath
Or eat a toadstool, instant death

The rich
Huddled outside the doors of their fallout shelters
Like drunken carolsingers
The poor
Clutching shattered televisions
And last week's editions of T.V. Times
(But the very last)

Civil defence volunteers
With their tin hats in one hand
And their heads in the other

C.N.D. supporters
Their ban the bomb badges beginning to rust
Have scrawled 'I told you so' in the dust

A littlebit of heaven fell
From out the sky one day
It landed in Vermont
North-Eastern U.S.A.
The general at the radar screen
He should have got the sack
But that wouldn't bring
Three thousand million, seven hundred,
and sixty-eight people back,
Would it?

109. Your Attention Please   *Peter Porter*

The Polar DEW[1] has just warned that
A nuclear rocket strike of
At least one thousand megatons[2]
Has been launched by the enemy
Directly at our major cities.
This announcement will take
Two and a quarter minutes to make,
You therefore have a further
Eight and a quarter minutes
To comply with the shelter
Requirements published in the Civil
Defence Code – section Atomic Attack.
A specially shortened Mass
Will be broadcast at the end
Of this announcement –

The Last Dawn But One by Jack B. Yeats (National Gallery of Ireland)

Protestant and Jewish Services
Will begin simultaneously –
Select your wavelength immediately
According to instructions
In the Defence Code. Do not
Take well-loved pets (including birds)
Into your shelter – they will consume
Fresh air. Leave the old and bed-
Ridden, you can do nothing for them.
Remember to press the sealing
Switch when everyone is in
The shelter. Set the radiation
Aerial, turn on the geiger barometer[3]
Turn off your Television now.

Turn off your radio immediately
The Services end. At the same time
Secure explosion plugs in the ears
Of each member of your family. Take
Down your plasma[4] flasks. Give your children
The pills marked one and two
In the C.D. green container, then put
Them to bed. Do not break
The inside airlock seals until
The radiation All Clear shows
(Watch for the cuckoo in our
Perspex panel), or your District
Touring Doctor rings your bell.
If before this your air becomes
Exhausted or if any of your family
Is critically injured, administer
The capsules marked 'Valley Forge'[5]
(Red pocket in No. I Survival Kit)
For painless death. (Catholics
Will have been instructed by their priests
What to do in this eventuality.)
This announcement is ending. Our President
Has already given orders for
Massive retaliation – it will be
Decisive. Some of us may die.
Remember, statistically
It is not likely to be you.
All flags are flying fully dressed
On Government buildings – the sun is shining.
Death is the least we have to fear.
We are all in the hands of God,
Whatever happens happens by His Will.
Now go quickly to your shelters.

1 Direct Early Warning radar station
2 Explosive force of 1,000,000 tons of TNT
3 Device for detecting radio-activity
4 Blood for transfusion
5 American government Defence suppliers

SECTION H
THOUGHTS FOR TODAY

110. Five Ways to Kill a Man

Edwin Brock

There are many cumbersome ways to kill a man.
You can make him carry a plank of wood
to the top of a hill and nail him to it. To do this
properly you require a crowd of people
wearing sandals, a cock that crows, a cloak
to dissect, a sponge, some vinegar and one
man to hammer the nails home.

Or you can take a length of steel,
shaped and chased in a traditional way,
and attempt to pierce the metal cage he wears.
But for this you need white horses,
English trees, men with bows and arrows,
at least two flags, a prince, and a
castle to hold your banquet in.

Dispensing with nobility, you may, if the wind
allows, blow gas at him. But then you need
a mile of mud sliced through with ditches,
not to mention black boots, bomb craters,
more mud, a plague of rats, a dozen songs
and some round hats made of steel.

In an age of aeroplanes, you may fly
miles above your victim and dispose of him by
pressing one small switch. All you then
require is an ocean to separate you, two
systems of government, a nation's scientists,
several factories, a psychopath and
land that no-one needs for several years.

These are, as I began, cumbersome ways
to kill a man. Simpler, direct, and much more neat
is to see that he is living somewhere in the middle
of the twentieth century, and leave him there.

111. One in Ten

UB40

I am the one in ten, a number on a list;
I am the one in ten, even though I don't exist.
Nobody knows me, though I'm always there,
A statistical reminder of a world that doesn't care.

My arms enfold the dole queue,
    Malnutrition dulls my hair,
My eyes are black and lifeless
    With an underprivileged stare;
I'm the beggar on the corner,
    Will no one spare a dime?
I'm the child that never learns to read
    'Cause no one spared the time.
I'm the murderer, the victim,
    I'm licensed with a gun,
I'm the sad and bruised old lady
    In an alley, in a slum;
I'm a middle-aged businessman
    With chronic heart disease,
I'm another teenage suicide
    In a street that has no trees;
I'm a starving Third World mother
    A refugee without a home,
I'm a housewife hooked on valium,
    I'm a pensioner alone;
I'm a cancer-ridden spectre,
    Covering the earth,
I'm another hungry baby,
    I'm an accident of birth.

112. Girls in a Factory

Denis Glover

Seated in rows at the machines
Their heads are bent; the tacking needle
Stitches along the hours, along the seams.

What thoughts follow the needle
Over the fields of cloth,
Stitching into the seams
Perhaps a scarlet thread of love,
A daisy-chain of dreams?

113. Film Star   *Ian Serraillier*

He was a rich pin-up boy – Mercedes, plane, etc.
His smile, like the winter sun, was bright,
But didn't warm you. One side of his face
Was handsome – the side that caught the light
    In front of the cameras.

And all the girls adored him.

His days were a whirlwind of wonders: he fell off
Mountains, jumped out of the sky, fought
With twenty at a time, went down with his ship
Smiling – it was all the bravest sport –
    In front of the cameras.

And all the girls adored him.

But was the smile his own? Yes, but never
The danger. That burning driver in the prairie race
Was another man. Where was the rich pin-up boy then?
Reading his newspaper in a safer place –
    Behind the cameras.

And all the girls adored him.

Weeks later, on his way to the studio, he crashed
His Mercedes, cut his face (the handsome side). O cruel blow!
Fifteen days he lay on his back, a little boy
Frightened of the dark, crying for mother. He wouldn't go
    In front of the cameras.

And all the girls forgot him.

114. ADMAN *Nigel Gray*

I'm the new man
in the ivory tower
the new man
the man with the power
the old village chief
used to lay down the law
but the medicine man
had his foot in the door
he taught me the secret
of how you tick
to use psychology
like a conjuring trick
so I've found the doorway
into your brain
when you get a bargain
you lose – I gain
I can get in your bath
I can get in your bed
I can get in your pants
I can get in your head
you're like a man on the cross
you're like a priest at the stake
you're like a fish on a hook
make no mistake
I can tie you up
I can take you down
I can sit and watch
you wriggle around
'cos I'm the medicine man
with the media touch
the man with the power that's
too much

115. EXECUTIVE *John Betjeman*

I am a young executive. No cuffs than mine are cleaner;
I have a Slimline brief-case and I use the firm's Cortina.
In every roadside hostelry from here to Burgess Hill
The *maîtres d'hôtel* all know me well and let me sign the bill.

You ask me what it is I do. Well actually, you know,
I'm partly a liaison man and partly P.R.O.
Essentially I integrate the current export drive
And basically I'm viable from ten o'clock till five.

For vital off-the-record work – that's talking transport-wise –
I've a scarlet Aston-Martin – and does she go? She flies!
Pedestrians and dogs and cats – we mark them down for slaughter.
I also own a speed-boat which has never touched the water.

She's built of fibre-glass, of course. I call her 'Mandy Jane'
After a bird I used to know – No soda, please, just plain –
And how did I acquire her? Well to tell you about that
And to put you in the picture I must wear my other hat.

I do some mild developing. The sort of place I need
Is a quiet country market town that's rather run to seed.
A luncheon and a drink or two, a little *savoir faire* –
I fix the Planning Officer, the Town Clerk and the Mayor.

And if some preservationist attempts to interfere
A 'dangerous structure' notice from the Borough Engineer
Will settle any buildings that are standing in our way –
The modern style, sir, with respect, has really come to stay.

116. HAPPINESS *Carl Sandburg*

I asked professors who teach the meaning of life to
    tell me what is happiness.
And I went to famous executives who boss the work of
    thousands of men.
They all shook their heads and gave me a smile as though
    I was trying to fool with them.
And then one Sunday afternoon I wandered out along the
    Desplaines* river
And I saw a crowd of Hungarians under the trees with
    their women and children and a keg of beer and an accordian.

* in Chicago, U.S.A.

117. CULTIVATORS
Susan Taylor

    We,
who work with earth and steel
and feel winter frozen in our hands
where fields are looms,
weave the patterns of crops;
damp loam flows like silk
through shuttling metal.

    And our hills,
with their wild uncurable wills
may be hard to till
but are easy to love,
steep work weakens the tractor
but strengthens the heart.

118. In My Country

In my country they jail you
for what they think you think.
My uncle once said to me:
they'll implant a microchip
in our minds
to flash our thoughts and dreams
on to a screen at John Vorster Square.
I was scared:
by day I guard my tongue
by night my dreams.

Pitika Ntuli (Azania)

119. Grandpa

*Paul Chidyausiku
(Zimbabwe)*

They say they are healthier than me
Though they can't walk to the end of a mile;
At their age I walked forty at night
To wage a battle at dawn.

They think they are healthier than me:
If their socks get wet they catch a cold;
When my sockless feet got wet, I never sneezed –
But they still think they are healthier than me.

On a soft mattress over a spring bed,
They still have to take a sleeping-pill:
But I, with reeds cutting into my ribs,
My head resting on a piece of wood,
I sleep like a babe and snore.

They blow their noses and pocket the stuff –
That's hygienic so they tell me:
I blow my nose into the fire,
But they say that is barbaric.

If a dear one dies I weep without shame;
If someone jokes I laugh with all my heart.
They stifle a tear as if to cry was something wrong,
But they also stifle a laugh,
As if to laugh was something wrong, too.
No wonder they need psychiatrists!

They think they have more power of will than me.
Our women were scarcely covered in days of yore,
But adultery was a thing unknown:
Today they go wild on seeing a slip on a hanger!

When I have more than one wife
They tell me that hell is my destination
But when they have one and countless mistresses,
They pride themselves on cheating the world!

No, let them learn to be honest with themselves first
Before they persuade me to change my ways,
Says my grandfather, the proud old man.

Paul Durcan **120. WHAT IS A PROTESTANT, DADDY?**

Gaiters were sinister
And you dared not
Glance up at the visage;
It was a long lean visage
With a crooked nose
And beaked dry lips
And streaky gray hair
And they used scurry about
In small black cars
(Unlike Catholic bishops
Stately in big cars
Or Pope Pius XII
In his gold-plated Cadillac)

And they'd make dashes for it
Across deserted streets
And disappear quickly
Into vast cathedrals
All silent and aloof,
Forlorn and leafless,
Their belfry louvres
Like dead men's lips,
And whose congregations, if any,
Were all octogenarian
With names like Iris;
More likely
There were no congregations
And these rodent-like clergymen
Were conspirators;
You could see it in their faces;
But as to what the conspiracies
Were about, as children
We were at a loss to know;
Our parents called them 'parsons'
Which turned them from being rodents
Into black hooded crows
Evilly flapping their wings
About our virginal souls;
And these 'parsons' had wives –
As unimaginable a state of affairs
As it would have been to imagine
A pope in a urinal;
Protestants were Martians
Light-years more weird
Than zoological creatures;
But soon they would all go away
For as a species they were dying out.
Soon there would be no more Protestants. . .
O Yea, O Lord,
I was a proper little Irish Catholic boy
Way back in the 1950s.

121. FROM THE IRISH

James Simmons

Most terrible was our hero in battle blows:
hands without fingers, shorn heads and toes
were scattered. That day there flew and fell
from astonished victims eyebrow, bone and entrail,
like stars in the sky, like snowflakes, like nuts in May,
like a meadow of daisies, like butts from an ashtray.

Familiar things, you might brush against or tread
upon in a daily round, were glistening red
with the slaughter the hero caused, though he had gone.
By proxy his bomb exploded, his valour shone.

122. MISSIONARY

D.M. Thomas

A harsh entry I had of it, Grasud;*
the tiny shuttle strained to its limits
by radiation-belts, dust-storms,
not to mention the pitiless heat which
hit it on plunging into the atmosphere
— its fire-shield clean vaporised; and then,

* spoken by an alien from another part of the universe

on landing, the utter cold and stillness
of a mountain-slope, cedar-trees and
what they call
snow. As I went numbly through the
routine I could do in my sleep –
mentalising myself, smothering
my body and the shuttle in a
defensive neutrino-screen, hiding them
securely in the snow,
I looked up and, between the branches
of the cedars, could see
the mother-ship sliding away through
the dark, like an unfixed star, westwards
to its other destinations: that was
the worst moment of all, Grasud! I'd have
called it back! So lonely, such an alien
world they'd left me in. Goodbye, Lagash!
goodbye, Theremon! fare well! (But no
voice now even to make a gesture against
the silence.)
    Then the agonisingly slow
descent, towards the village,
my spirit dark, already missing
not only Theremon and Lagash, but
that other friend, my body's familiar
chemistry. By now I felt my
vaunted courage ebbing, Grasud; I think
those years of training
alone forced me to go on, into the village,
into the houses, inns, into
— after much vain searching – a ripened
womb; there superseding
(not without a pang) its foetus-spirit.
How black that airlock,
after the six suns of our own system,
I needn't tell you. Even space,
in recollection, seemed a blaze of

supernovas.* But I settled to my task
wrestling to get on terms with carbon
compounds fearsomely different from
the synthetic ones I'd practised in.
Of course, as I was born and the years
passed, it seemed as natural to go
on man's two legs as on our Vardian
limbs. But when these pains eased,
one far bitterer grew: my seeds were cast
on stony ground; the more
I exhorted,
—the more I spoke, obliquely of
the many mansions of our Vardian
Commonwealth, and of the place
that could be theirs – the more it
seemed those simple, instinctive creatures
lied, stole, slandered, fornicated,
killed. . . . Grasud, how often, sick with
failure, only the words of Vrak
sustained me – 'a world lies in your hands.'
That was the time he
sent for the three of us when
all ears were ringing with the news of
the three life-planets found in
NDT 1065. If we had hopes,
we masked them. His words to us, for
all that's happened, I'll hoard always.
'Thoorin, Lagash, Theremon,' I hear him
saying, 'I'm sending *you*. . . . you're young,
but this is what you've trained for, bio-
enlightenment. You've done well.'
And then – 'a world lies in your hands.'
So, Grasud, I toiled. In the end
I tried too hard; the time of space –
rendezvous was almost come. Anyway
they killed me. I loved them, and they
killed me.

Yes, it was hard,
as you can well imagine,
on the return-journey, to avoid feeling
the faintest warp of
jealousy, as Theremon and
Lagash talked with
the happy emissaries of their
planets. – What does Vrak say? He is
kind, promises – after this loathsome
rest – another
chance, though not of course on that
planet. My 'inability' (he avoids
the word failure) to raise them
ethically to the point where we could
safely announce ourselves, proves, he
says, there's no point trying again
for a few thousand years. Meanwhile,
he suggests, maybe some of my words
will start to bear fruit. . . . He is kind!
His last words were 'Forget about it,
Thoorin; enjoy your stay on
Atar.' Forget!
with the relaxed faces of my friends a
perpetual thorn!

* very bright stars.

John Lennon and Paul McCartney

123. LET IT BE

When I find myself in times of trouble Mother Mary comes to me
Speaking words of wisdom, Let it be.
And in my hour of darkness she is standing right in front of me
Speaking words of wisdom, Let it be.
Let it be, Let it be, Let it be, Let it be, whisper words of wisdom,
Let it be.

And when the broken hearted people living in the world agree
There will be an answer, Let it be.
For though they may be parted there is still a chance that they will
    see,
There will be an answer, Let it be.
Let it be, Let it be, Let it be, Let it be, there will be an answer,
Let it be.

And when the night is cloudy, there is still a light that shines on me,
Shine until tomorrow, Let it be.
I wake up to the sound of music, Mother Mary comes to me,
Speaking words of wisdom, Let it be.
Let it be, Let it be, Let it be, Let it be, whisper words of wisdom,
Let it be.

124. God's Grandeur

Gerard Manley Hopkins

The world is charged with the grandeur of God.
    It will flame out, like shining from shook foil;
    It gathers to a greatness, like the ooze of oil
Crushed. Why do men then now not reck his rod?
Generations have trod, have trod, have trod;
    And all is seared with trade; bleared, smeared with toil;
    And wears man's smudge and shares man's smell: the soil
Is bare now, nor can foot feel, being shod.

And for all this, nature is never spent;
    There lives the dearest freshness deep down things;
And though the last lights off the black West went
    Oh, morning, at the brown brink eastward, springs –
Because the Holy Ghost over the bent
    World broods with warm breast and with ah! bright wings.

125. Desiderata

Max Ehrmann

'Go placidly amid the noise and the haste, and remember what peace there may be in silence. As far as possible without surrender be on good terms with all persons. Speak your truth quietly and clearly; and listen to others, even the dull and ignorant; they too have their story. Avoid loud and aggressive persons, they are vexatious to the spirit. If you compare yourself with others you may become vain and bitter; for always there will be greater and lesser persons than yourself. Enjoy your achievements as well as your plans. Keep interested in your own career, however humble; it is a real possession in the changing fortunes of time. Exercise caution in your business affairs; for the world is full of trickery. But let this not blind you to what virtue there is; many persons strive for high ideals; and everywhere life is full of heroism. Be yourself. Especially do not feign affection. Neither be cynical about love; for in the face of all aridity and disenchantment it is as perennial as the grass. Take kindly the counsel of the years, gracefully surrendering the things of youth. Nurture strength of spirit to shield you in sudden misfortune. But do not distress yourself with imaginings. Many fears are born of fatigue and loneliness. Beyond a wholesome discipline, be gentle with yourself. You are a child of the universe no less than the trees and the stars; you have a right to be here. And whether or not it is clear to you, no doubt the universe is unfolding as it should. Therefore be at peace with God, whatever you conceive Him to be. And whatever your labours and aspirations, in the noisy confusion of life keep peace with your soul. With all its sham, drudgery and broken dreams, it is still a beautiful world. Be cheerful. Strive to be happy.'

SECTION I
TAKING YOUR PEN FOR A WALK

The Greek word for poet was *poietes*, meaning a MAKER or an author. The Anglo-Saxon word was *scop*, meaning a SHAPER. So rather than think of the poet as a strange, moody, specially-gifted person, who is galvanised into writing by the lighting strike of inspiration, it is more accurate to see the poet as a craftsperson, a shaper of words. We are, all of us, shapers of words. We all can try our hand at the craft of poetry.

The poet, like any good craftsperson, has his or her techniques or tricks of the trade. One technique which poets rely on to get their ideas across is that of making images.

> **IMAGE**: An image is a mental picture which the poet creates for us with words. It is usually very clear or vivid and we can easily imagine it if we close our eyes.
>
> *For example:* When *Wes Magee* speaks of himself as an adolescent in *'Growing Up?' (No. 8)* on the verge of independence, he asks:
> 'Can it be
> that it's happened,
> that I'm ready
> to step out of my cage?'

EXERCISES
1. Think of all the suggestions or connotations that Wes Magee's image conjures up for the reader. List them.
2. Re-read a favourite poem and examine the images you find.

> **SIMILE**: This is a type of image or verbal picture made simply by comparing two things, using the words 'like', 'as' or 'than'.
> *For example:*
> 'A line of elms plunging and tossing like horses'
> *Theodore Roethke, 'Child on Top of a Greenhouse' (No. 3)*

EXERCISES
1. Complete the following similes and compare notes for originality and effectiveness.
    (a) The dawn came up like . . .
    (b) The sound of the ice breaking was as . . .
    (c) The teacher's car is as . . .

(d) My young brother eats like . . .
   (e) My sister's cooking tastes like . . .
   (f) After the motorway, the sounds of the wood were as . . .
   (g) School is noiser than . . .
2. Create similes to describe: a snow-covered tree; a cold shower; the view from a tossing boat; a difficult exam question; the voice of a DJ or newsreader; a character from a 'soap' you watch.
3. Examine some simile poem such as 'Winter' by L. A. G. Strong (No. 47).

> **METAPHOR**: A slightly more complex and subtle image, created by comparing two things, without using the words 'like', 'as' or 'than'.
> *For example*:
> 'Slant and curved the word-swords fall to pierce and stick inside me'.
> *'Truth', Barrie Wade (No. 22)*

EXERCISES
1. What is the comparison in 'Truth' and what does it suggest?
2. 'Night is the smashing of a light bulb. Failure is a dagger in your heart.' Simon Sloan (aged 13).
   Complete the following:
   (a) Dawn is . . .
   (b) Success is . . .
   (c) Reading is . . .
   (d) Skateboarding is . . .
   (e) Windsurfing is . . .
   (f) Music is . . .
   (g) Friday evenings are . . .
   (h) Friends are . . .
   (i) Roads are . . .

The Anglo-Saxon poets were good at making metaphors, which they called KENNINGS. *For example*: The sea was described as 'the whale's road'.

   Wind – 'howl of the dying wolf'
   God – 'the ordainer of fate'

EXERCISE

Create kennings for: thunder, snow, rain, cat, horse, doctor, teacher, priest, nurse, accountant etc.

A good kenning should catch the essential nature of the object.

The metaphysical poets of the seventeenth century used a kind of metaphor called a CONCEIT, where the comparison was more startling than accurate. Can you find any examples of these?

Some metaphors are simple, single images; others are longer and more complex. These extended metaphors can take up an entire poem, as in this next example.

Julie O'Callaghan

126. TAKING MY PEN FOR A WALK

Tonight I took the leash off my pen.
At first it was frightened,
looked up at me with confused eyes, tongue panting.
Then I said, 'Go on, run away,'
and pushed its head.
Still it wasn't sure what I wanted;
it whimpered with its tail between its legs.
So I yelled, 'You're free, why don't you run –
you stupid pen, you should be glad.
Now get out of my sight.'
It took a few steps.
I stamped my foot and threw a stone.
Suddenly, it realised what I was saying
and began to run furiously away from me.

EXERCISES
1. In using this metaphor, what do you think the poet is trying to say about writing?
2. Find and read some of the other metaphor poems in this book, such as: 'To Waken an Old Lady', William Carlos Williams, No. 86; or 'Fog', Carl Sandburg, No. 42; or 'Crossing the Bar', Tennyson, No. 90.

127. ONE WAY OF FLYING *James Kirkup*

As in a dream, you need
no machine, or shrieking jet –
no take-off or landing
need bother you at all.

You just push off from
nothing, into the dark rim
of outer space, wearing only
an eagle cap, boots, jumpsuit.

And all you need is wings of
fantasy like a butterfly bat's
and a sailship's rigging
on which to brace your feet.

Your arms, flung wide, as in sleep –
knees bent for the slalom of stars –
hands grip the membrane of a dream –
hang-glider of the haunted airs.

EXERCISES
1. What is the poet describing here?
2. Do you think it is a good metaphor? Why?
3. Make an image which expresses for you the most important thing about writing.
4. Did you notice James Kirkup's kenning for the poet: 'hang-glider of the haunted airs'?
   Compose kennings for a journalist; a novelist; a musician; a sculptor; a painter.
5. Did you notice the sound effects of some words?

> **ONOMATOPOEIA**: Where the sound of the word is similar to the meaning. For example, 'the shrieking jet'.
> Did you ever hear the high pitched sound of a jet engine revving up?
> **ALLITERATION**: Where two or more words in close connection begin with the same letter or sound. For example, 'the slalom of stars'. Notice how the alliteration creates a kind of beat by emphasising the opening sounds in the two words.

In the following poem 'I Hear . . .', Berlie Doherty catches the sounds of school. Examine how she does it.

Berlie Doherty

128. I Hear......

When I think of school
I hear
High shouts tossed
Like juggled balls in windy yards, and lost
In gutters, treetops, all.
And always, somewhere.
Piano-notes water-fall
And small sharp voices wail.
A monster-roar surges – 'Goal!'.
The bell.
Then doors slam. There's the kick, scuff, stamp of shoes
Down corridors that trap and trail echoes.
Desk-tops thud with books, kit-bags,
A child's ghost screams as her chair's pushed back.
Laughter bubbles up and bursts.
Screech-owl whistles. Quick-fox quarrel-flares.
The voice barks 'QUIET!'
All sit. All wait.
Till scraped chalk shrieks
And whispers creep.
Cough. Ruler crack. Desk creak.
And furtive into the silence comes
A tiny mouse-scrabbling of pens.
Scamper. Stop. Scamper. Stop. Tiptoe
And there, just outside the top window
As if it had never ceased to be
But only needed listening to
A scatter of birdsong, floating free.

129. AFTER ENGLISH CLASS

Jean Little

I used to like 'Stopping by Woods on a Snowy Evening.'
I liked the coming darkness,
The jingle of harness bells, breaking – and adding to – the stillness,
the gentle drift of snow . . .

But today, the teacher told us what everything stood for.
The woods, the horse, the miles to go, the sleep –
They all have 'hidden meanings.'

It's grown so complicated now that,
Next time I drive by,
I don't think I'll bother to stop.

EXERCISES
1. Read Robert Frost's poem again (No. 48). Then think about this one. Do you know what the poet is talking about here?
2. Did you ever have this experience with a poem?
3. Listen to 'Colours' by Harry Chapin.

130. TIMELY

Christopher Nolan

I got a Micro-processor,
My Mother hangs around,
She forgets that I can operate
Without her efforts now.
Nobody can imagine,
My escape route from despair,
It came from many nations,
Who read *The Times* as
Sunday prayer. The surplus
Money may provide many mighty
Mesmerising dreams, for
Handicapped – imprisoned, isolated,
Tongue-tied, to feel welcomed
By the world – released.

The Sunday Times launched an appeal for funds to purchase a computer for me. The appeal was a huge success. The Handicapped

Children's Aid Committee of London presented me with the complete unit. It was at this stage that the Christopher Nolan Trust was set up, and all surplus funds from the appeal were at my request allocated to the providing of computerised equipment for other tongue-tied, disabled people.

9 March 1980

EXERCISES
1. Do you know of the work of any other disabled artists or writers? Talk about it with your class.
2. Listen to 'I'm free', by The Who.

131. POEM TO BE BURIED IN A TIME CAPSULE *James Kirkup*

My poem is in itself
a kind of time capsule.
It contains my essence,
my native speech,
my choice of words,
my thought, my laughter
and my very breath.

You can swallow it
like a vitamin pill –
one that you absorb
through eyes and ears,
until your own lungs,
throat, tongue and lips
reconstitute its voice.

Through its lines you hear
my own voice speaking
across the centuries.
Though I have long been dead,
this poem is a living thing
from secret sources
that are living still.

Be careful as you
unearth my mystery; and
unwind my age-old wrappings
tenderly, with understanding
of my fragility, that hides
an unsuspected toughness
preserving precious seeds.

— Because a time capsule poem
is also a kind of time bomb
whose delayed-action meanings
can only be safely defused
by those who learn to read
between the lines. – Otherwise
I self-destruct! So mind what you do.

EXERCISES
1. In pairs, discuss the extended metaphor in this poem. Is it a good one? How well does it match etc.?
2. What do you suppose the poet might mean by the 'secret sources' of verse 3?
3. Have you ever experienced any of the 'delayed-action meanings' he mentions in verse 5?
4. Write your own time capsule poem. It should be a fairly personal poem which will carry something of you through the ages. It could be:
   (a) About a memory or an incident which was important to you, an autobiographical poem.
   (b) About a family member or a friend or an interesting character you know.
   (c) About your town or countryside – a street scene or a view you see every day. Think about it as a photograph and then write about it.
   (d) About a season you like or a school event.
   (e) About any aspect of Irish life and culture.
   (f) If you feel uncomfortable with a poem, then write a diary extract for a day in your life. Read the first verse again. Think in images.
5. Perhaps all the poems could be put in a class capsule, to be kept until you are leaving school!

SOME HINTS
1. Think in images and just jot down phrases. Let images rather than full sentences carry the meaning.
2. It might be useful to think of the subject as a photograph – whether landscape, still life, or action still. Try to catch the essence of that scene.
* Go through the senses: colours, sounds, touch/texture, smells etc. Is there anything unusual you wish to note and describe?
* Consider the relationship between objects or between people in the photograph. Is there anything unusual or interesting about it?
* How do you feel about the scene? Will the reader know how you feel from the language, images etc.? Does the poem express the tone you want?

Here is a nature poem, constructed as if each verse was a photograph of a month of the year.

132. JANUARY TO DECEMBER   *Patricia Beer*

The warm cows have gone
From the fields where grass stands up
Dead-alive like steel.

Unexpected sun
Probes the house as if someone
Had left the lights on.

Novel no longer
Snowdrops melt in the hedge, drain
Away into spring.

The heron shining
Works his way up the bright air
Above the river.

Earth dries. The sow basks
Flat out with her blue-black young,
Ears over their eyes.

The early lambs, still
Fleecy, look bulkier now
Than their shorn mothers.

In this valley full
Of bird song, the gap closes
Behind the cuckoo.

Fields of barley glimpsed
Through trees shine out like golden
Windows in winter.

Though nothing has changed –
The sun is even hotter –
Death is in the air.

Long shadows herald
Or dog every walker
In the cut-back lanes.

A crop of mist grows
Softly in the valley, lolls
Over the strawstacks.

Meadows filmed across
With rain stare up at winter
Hardening in the hills.

You can practise by using any of the photographs in this book.

POETIC FORMS

If you wish to shape your poem into a particular form, you might try one of these.

THE HAIKU

This is a Japanese form of poetry where the writer tries to capture the mood of something in three short lines. The first and third lines should have five syllables each and the second line should have seven.

EXAMPLES

Haikus
They are short poems
They've seventeen syllables
In three lines only
Keith Keogh (12)

New Calf
The new calf lies down
His caring mother watches
Never a closed eye
Brendan Barret (12)

Church Bells
Singing of angels
Soft as gentle whispering
Sweeter than God's voice
Ronan Hickey (12)

A Stranded Jellyfish
Squirming like a worm
Knowing death is near to him
People going 'ugh'!
Niall Manley (12)

Now try some Haikus on: an old tree; crows; a footprint on the sand; cats at night; snow in the school yard – or any other subject that interests you.

THE TANKA

THE TANKA has five lines, with 5, 7, 5, 7, 7 syllables respectively. So you can make your Haiku into a Tanka by adding two lines of 7 syllables each.

EXAMPLE

At the Local
In the public house
old men with strong oaken hands
finger dominoes,
small oblong nights of white stars.
We hear the click of old bones.

THE CINQUAIN
THE CINQUAIN also has five lines, with 2, 4, 6, 8, 2 syllables respectively. It can also be structured according to the number of words per line, with 1, 2, 3, 4 and 1 word respectively.

Try some Haikus, Tankas and Cinquains and see which form you prefer.

THE LIMERICK
THE LIMERICK has five lines and a rhyming scheme aabba. The 1st, 2nd and 5th lines usually have three stressed syllables each, and the 3rd and 4th are usually shorter two-stress lines.

EXAMPLES

The bottle of perfume that Willie sent	a
Was highly displeasing to Millicent	a
Her thanks were so cold	b
They quarrelled, I'm told	b
Through the silly scent Willie sent Millicent	a

(*Anon.*)

There once was a boy from Clonkeen
Whose mum said, 'Where have you been?'
'I got one hour's detention
And two days' suspension,
'Cos the teachers are horrid and mean.'
Ian McPartland (13)

There was a young bard of Japan
Whose limericks never would scan;
When told it was so,
He said: 'Yes, I know,
But I always try and get as many words into the last line as I possibly can.'

Try some Limericks beginning

> There was a young fellow called Pete . . .
> There was a young lady of Spain . . .
> There was an old man of Harrow . . .
> A wicked old witch of the West . . .
> A grumpy old bear at the zoo . . .

If you can manage a more complex poetic form, then try a SONNET. See pages 138–39, 164 and 173 for information on the Italian and English forms. For a modern sonnet, see 'High Flight' by John Magee (No. 27).

Patrick Kavanagh

133. PEGASUS

My soul was an old horse
Offered for sale in twenty fairs.
I offered him to the Church – the buyers
Were little men who feared his unusual airs.
One said: 'Let him remain unbid
In the wind and rain and hunger
Of sin and we will get him –
With the winkers thrown in – for nothing.'

Then the men of State looked at
What I'd brought for sale.
One minister, wondering if
Another horse-body would fit the tail
That he'd kept for sentiment –
The relic of his own soul –
Said, 'I will graze him in lieu of his labour.'
I lent him for a week or more
And he came back a hurdle of bones,
Starved, overworked, in despair.
I nursed him on the roadside grass
To shape him for another fair.

I lowered my price. I stood him where
The broken-winded, spavined stand
And crooked shopkeepers said that he
Might do a season on the land –
But not for high-paid work in towns.
He'd do a tinker, possibly.
I begged, 'O make some offer now,
A soul is a poor man's tragedy.
He'll draw your dungiest cart,' I said,
'Show you short cuts to Mass,
Teach weather lore, at night collect
Bad debts from poor men's grass.'
                         And they would not.

        Where the
Tinkers quarrel I went down
With my horse, my soul.
I cried, 'Who will bid me half a crown?'
From their rowdy bargaining
Not one turned. 'Soul,' I prayed,
'I have hawked you through the world
Of Church and State and meanest trade.
But this evening, halter off,
Never again will it go on.
On the south side of ditches
There is grazing of the sun.
No more haggling with the world . . . .'

As I said these words he grew
Wings upon his back. Now I may ride him
Every land my imagination knew.

In pairs or small groups, discuss what this poem says about the attitude of society to the poet. What is your idea of the role or importance of the poet, singer or artist in society? REPORT BACK.

Dylan Thomas   **134. IN MY CRAFT OR SULLEN ART**

In my craft or sullen art
Exercised in the still night
When only the moon rages
And the lovers lie abed
With all their griefs in their arms,
I labour by singing light
Not for ambition or bread
Or the strut and trade of charms
On the ivory stages
But for the common wages
Of their most secret heart.

Not for the proud man apart
From the raging moon I write
On these spindrift pages
Nor for the towering dead
With their nightingales and psalms
But for the lovers, their arms
Round the griefs of the ages,
Who pay no praise or wages
Nor heed my craft or art.

According to Dylan Thomas, why does the poet write – what is his or her motivation? In your groups, discuss why people write. REPORT BACK.

Ted Hughes   **135. THE THOUGHT-FOX**

I imagine this midnight moment's forest:
Something else is alive
Beside the clock's loneliness
And this blank page where my fingers move.

Through the window I see no star:
Something more near
Though deeper within darkness
Is entering the loneliness:

Cold, delicately as the dark snow,
A fox's nose touches twig, leaf;
Two eyes serve a movement, that now
And again now, and now, and now

Sets neat prints into the snow
Between trees, and warily a lame
Shadow lags by stump and in hollow
Of a body that is bold to come

Across clearings, an eye,
A widening deepening greenness,
Brilliantly, concentratedly,
Coming about its own business

Till, with a sudden sharp hot stink of fox
It enters the dark hole of the head.
The window is starless still; the clock ticks,
The page is printed.

The Poet Comments

This poem does not have anything you could easily call a meaning. It is about a fox, obviously enough, but a fox that is both a fox and not a fox. What sort of a fox is it that can step right into my head where presumably it still sits . . . smiling to itself when the dogs bark. It is both a fox and a spirit. It is a real fox; as I read the poem I see it move, I see it setting its prints, I see its shadow going over the irregular surface of the snow. The words show me all this, bringing it nearer and nearer. It is very real to me. The words have made a body for it and given it somewhere to walk.

If, at the time of writing this poem, I had found livelier words, words that could give me much more vividly its movements, the twitch and craning of its ears, the slight tremor of its hanging tongue and its breath making little clouds, its teeth bared in the cold, the snow-crumbs dropping from its pads as it lifts each one in turn, if I could have got the words for all this, the fox would probably be even more real and alive to me now, than it is as I read the poem. Still, it is there as it is. If I had not caught the real fox there in the words I would never have saved the poem. I would have thrown it into the wastepaper basket as I have thrown so many other hunts that did not get what I was after. As it is, every time I read the poem the fox comes up again out of the darkness and steps into my head. And I suppose that long after I am gone, as long as a copy of the poems exists, every time anyone reads it the fox will get up somewhere out in the darkness and come walking towards them.

So, you see, in some ways my fox is better than an ordinary fox. It will live for ever, it will never suffer from hunger or hounds. I have it with me wherever I go. And I made it. And all through imagining it clearly enough and finding the living words.

Ted Hughes

This is a poem about writing a poem. Read it, together with the poet's comment, and discuss it in your groups. Notice how Hughes catches the essential details, movements, smells etc. of the fox.

Observe some animal closely or think about an animal you know well and write a poem about it. Read the poems in your groups.

STYLE

> Style refers to the distinctive, personal way in which a poet or any writer expresses ideas. One might notice choice of imagery; choice of words (diction); sounds; the rhythm or metre; the structuring of phrases and sentences (syntax) etc. These are some of the things which establish a poet's different or particular style.

You might like to consider the distinctive elements of style you find in the work of some of the following poets:

Seamus Heaney
'Mother of the Groom' (No. 18)
'Digging' (No. 19)
'Saint Francis and the Birds' (No. 34)
'The Diviner' (No. 54)
'Mid-term Break' (No. 83)

Roger McGough
'The Identification' (No. 84)
'Let Me Die a Youngman's Death' (No. 89)
'Icarus Allsorts' (No. 108)

W. B. Yeats
'He Wishes for the Cloths of Heaven' (No. 66)
'When you are Old' (No. 75)
'An Irish Airman Foresees His Death' (No. 96)

Mick Gowar
'Hero' (No. 23)
'King of the Kurzel' (No. 64)

Siegfried Sassoon
'The General' (No. 96)
'The Hero' (No. 101)

John Betjeman
'Diary of a Church Mouse' (No. 38)
'Executive' (No. 115)

D. M. Thomas
'Limbo' (No. 24)
'Missionary' (No. 122)

James Kirkup
'The Beautiful Strangers' (No. 62)
'One Way of Flying' (No. 127)

Kit Wright
'Hugger mugger' (No. 11)
'The Song of the Whale' (No. 52)

Harry Graham
'Indifference' (No. 12)
'Appreciation' (No. 13)
'Father' (No. 14)
'Tragedy' (No. 16)
'The Ideal Husband' (No. 74)

Julie O'Callaghan
'Edible Anecdote No. 24' (No. 25)
'Taking My Pen for a Walk' (No. 126)

Robert Frost
'The Road Not Taken' (No. 28)
'Stopping by Woods on a Snowy Evening' (No. 48)

Dylan Thomas
'Do not go gentle into that good night' (No. 91)
'In My Craft or Sullen Art' (No. 134)

William Wordsworth
'I Wandered Lonely As a Cloud' (No. 29)
'The World is Too Much With Us' (No. 57)
'She Dwelt Among the Untrodden Ways' (No. 85)

John Montague
'The Cage' (No. 20)
'The Trout' (No. 51)
'Like Dolmens Round my Childhood, the Old People' (No. 55)

Gareth Owen
'My Sister Betty' (No. 10)
'Space Shot' (No. 58)

Ted Hughes
'Sheep' (No. 39)
'The Thought-Fox' (No. 135)

Gerard Manley Hopkins
'Pied Beauty' (No. 30)
'Spring' (No. 45)
'God's Grandeur' (No. 124)

A PARODY is a work in which an author's style is ridiculed or made fun of by imitation. This parody may help you to see some of the elements of Hopkins' style.

136. BREAKFAST WITH GERARD MANLEY HOPKINS

Anthony Brode

Delicious heart-of-the corn, fresh-from-the-oven flakes are sparkled and spangled with sugar for a can't-be-resisted flavour.
Legend on a packet of breakfast cereal

Serious over my cereals I broke one breakfast my fast
    With something-to-read-searching retinas retained by
        print on a packet;
Sprung rhythm sprang, and I found (the mind fact-mining at last)
    An influence Father-Hopkins-fathered on the copy-writing
        racket.

Parenthesis-proud, bracket-bold, happiest with hyphens,
    The writers stagger intoxicated by terms, adjective-unsteadied –
Describing in graceless phrases fizzling like soda siphons
    All things crisp, crunchy, malted, tangy, sugared and shredded,

Far too, yes, too early we are urged to be purged, to savour
    Salt, malt and phosphates in English twisted and torn,
As, sparkled and spangled with sugar for a can't-be-resisted flavour,
    Come fresh-from-the-oven flakes direct from the heart of the
        corn.

EXERCISES:
1. Can you spot the elements of Hopkins' style which are parodied here?
2. Write a parody of any poem from the anthology. Even the Bard is open to parody, as you will see in the next poem.

137. NEW IMPROVED SONNET XVIII

Peter Titheradge

Shall I equate thee with a summer's day?
Thou art more valid and more meaningful:
A north-west airstream will devalue May,
And summer's mortgage is foreclosable:
Sometimes the sun is too intensive-phased,
And often is his gold down-marketed,
And every fare by next year's fare's erased,

By an inflation situation fed:
But thy eternal summer's index-linked,
Nor shalt thou thine exclusive image lack,
Nor rate thy life-expectancy extinct,
When hopefully thou'rt out in paperback,
    So long as I'm in print and men are human,
    This is thy life-insurance, I'm thy Pru-man.

METRE AND RHYTHM

In English pronunciation, some syllables are stressed and others left unstressed. In speaking any word of more than one syllable, we give more weight to one syllable than to the others. So we say:

yēs/ter/day

to/dāy

Tra/lēe

Kill/ār/ney.

These stresses produce the rhythm or beat in a line of poetry. The **pattern** of these stressed and unstressed syllables is known as the **metre**.

Each stressed syllable usually has one or more unstressed syllables around it. This grouping of syllables is known as a **foot**. The most commonly found are:

Name	Code	Example
iamb	∪ —	tŏdāy
trochee	— ∪	pānĭc
anapaest	∪ ∪ —	ĭntĕrrūpt
dactyl	— ∪ ∪	tēndĕrlў

But you might also find:

amphibrach	∪ — ∪	Can you find examples of these?
spondee	— —	
pyrrhic	∪ ∪	

When marking a line of poetry, first indicate the stressed syllables with a –, then fill in the unstressed symbols with a ∪. This is known as **scansion**.

Not all the feet in a line conform to the pattern, so the predominant foot gives its name to the metre.

EXAMPLE A
IAMBIC – 'HIGH FLIGHT', (NO. 27)

'Oh, I / have slipped / the sur / ly bonds / of earth

And danced / the skies / on laugh / ter sil / vered wings'

EXAMPLE B
TROCHAIC – 'TRUTH' (NO. 22)

'Sticks and / stones may / break my / bones

EXAMPLE C
ANAPAESTIC – 'THE BURIAL OF SIR JOHN MOORE AFTER CORUNNA' (NO. 94)

'Not a drum / was heard /, not a fu / neral note . . .' –

Lines of poetry, of course, can be long or short.
- **Monometer**:   1 foot per line: see 'Dog Exercising Man'   No.   36
- **Dimeter**:   2 feet per line: see 'Adman'   No.   114
- **Trimeter**:   3 feet per line: see 'Crossing the Bar'   No.   90
- **Tetrameter**:   4 feet per line: see 'Truth'   No.   22
- **Pentameter**:   5 feet per line: see 'High Flight'   No.   27

So the metre of 'High Flight' is iambic pentameter, the most popular metre found in poetry.
- **Hexameter**, also called Alexandrine, has 6 feet per line.
- **Blank Verse**: Consists of lines of iambic pentameter which have no end rhymes.
- **Free Verse**: Consists of lines which are not composed according to any metric principle.

RHYME
This is where two or more words have matching sounds. There are different kinds of rhyme:
- **End Rhyme** – occurs at the end of lines. Example: 'When grandmama fell off the *boat* / and couldn't swim (and wouldn't *float*)'.
- **Internal Rhyme** – when the rhyme occurs other than at the end. Example: 'And all is *seared* with trade, *bleared smeared* with toil'.
- **Full Rhyme** – where the two words are exactly alike except for the first consonants of each, as in *boat* and *float* above.
- **Off Rhyme** or **Slant Rhyme** – where the sounds are similar but not identical.

EXAMPLE
Oh, I am a battery hen,
On me back there's not a *germ*
I never scratched a farmyard
And I never pecked a *worm*

- **Masculine Rhyme** – in words of more than one syllable where the stressed syllable is the final one. Example:
    Where, when as death shall all the world sŭbdūe,
    Our love shall live, and later life rĕnēw.
- **Feminine Rhyme** – when the stressed syllable of the rhyming word is not the final one. Example:
    And, which made my sorrow grēatĕr
    I was left to tip the wāitĕr.

GLOSSARY OF POETIC TERMS

allegory: A story told under the guise of another. See 'Missionary', D.M. Thomas (No. 122).

alliteration: Where two or more words in close connection begin with the same letter or sound. *Example*: 'When weeds, in wheels, shoot long and lovely and lush' – 'Spring', Gerard Manley Hopkins (No. 45).

assonance: Where two or more words in close connection have the same vowel sound. *Example*: 'Come live with *me* and *be* my love' – 'The Passionate Shepherd to His Love', Christopher Marlowe (No. 69).

autobiographical: Giving details or memories of a writer's own life. See 'Like Dolmens Round my Childhood, the Old People', John Montague (No. 55).

ballad: A narrative poem usually dealing with love, death or war. See 'Lady Diamond', Unknown (No. 72). See also page 171.

blank verse: Lines of iambic pentameter which do not rhyme. See Rhyme section, page 136.

caricature: Where a picture or description of someone is exaggerated in order to appear ridiculous. See 'My Sister Betty', Gareth Owen (No. 10).

cinquain: A five-line poem with a set number of syllables or words per line. See page 125.

elegy: A sad song or poem, usually lamenting the dead. See 'Mid-term Break', Seamus Heaney (No. 83); 'The Identification', Roger McGough (No. 84); 'She Dwelt Among the Untrodden Ways', William Wordsworth (No. 88); and others.

epic: Very long narrative poem, usually about the heroic exploits of some great figure from history or mythology. *Examples*: Homer's 'Iliad' and 'Odyssey' from classical Greece and Rome; and Milton's 'Paradise Lost' from seventeenth century England.

feet: The units of beat or rhythm in a line of poetry. See Metre section, page 134.

free verse: Lines of poetry which are not composed according to any metric principles.

haiku: Three-line poem of Japanese origin. See page 124.

hyperbole: Exaggeration.

image: Mental picture which the poet creates with words. See page 115. Simile and metaphor are types of image.

irony: *Verbal irony* means saying one thing but meaning another. *Example*:
Within the human world I know
Such goings on could not be so,
For human beings only do
What their religion tells them to.
'Diary of a Church Mouse', John Betjeman (No. 85)
See also 'From the Irish', James Simmons (No. 121)

Situational irony deals with the difference between what appears to be taking place and what does in fact happen. See 'My Sister Betty', Gareth Owen (No. 10).

limerick: Five-line rhyming poem. See page 125.

lyric: Any short poem conveying the deep personal feelings and emotions of the writer. It used to be written with regular metre and rhyme. The term is also used to describe the words of a song.

metaphor: A type of image where two things are compared without using the words 'like', 'as' or 'than'. *Example:* 'Their eyes are onions of despair' – 'The Boys of Winter', Alan Bold (No. 5). See also page 116.

metre: The beat or rhythm of a line. See Metre section, page 134.

mood: The feelings or attitude of the poet which come across through the words. See Tone, page 139.

narrative: A piece which tells a story. See the ballad 'Lady Diamond', (No. 72); 'Missionary', D.M. Thomas (No. 122).

ode: Originally meant to be sung, it is a slightly longer, more solemn poem, often dealing with philosophical issues such as justice, truth, solitude, immortality, art etc. See 'To Autumn', John Keats (No. 46).

onomatopoeia: Where the sound of the word is very close to the meaning. *Example:* 'The tick-tock of the clock'.

paradox: Apparent contradiction – a statement which seems contradictory or absurd on first reading, but which has a kernel of truth in it when studied.

parody: A work in which an author's style is made fun of by imitation. See 'The Passionate Astronaut to His Love', Greg Smenda (No. 69); 'Breakfast with Gerard Manley Hopkins' Anthony Brode (No. 136); 'New Improved Sonnet XVIII', Peter Titheradge (No. 137).

pathetic fallacy: When inanimate objects are described as if they were human, with feelings etc. See 'The River God', Stevie Smith (No. 53).

quatrain: A four-line verse or section of a poem.

refrain: Repeated lines or chorus.

rhyme: Where two or more words have matching sounds. See Rhyme section, page 136.

rhythm: Beat. See Metre, page 134.

satire: A work which attacks faults in people or society by mockery and cutting humour. See 'The General', Siegfried Sassoon (No. 99); 'Your Attention Please', Peter Porter (No. 109); 'Adman', Nigel Gray (No. 114); 'Executive', John Betjeman (No. 115).

scansion: Working a line of poetry into feet, to find the rhythm or metre.

simile: A type of image where two things are directly compared, using the words 'like', 'as' or 'than'. *Example:* 'as daft as a coot'.

sonnet: A fourteen-line poem with a strict rhyming scheme. There are two main types: Petrarchan and Shakespearean. For details see pages 164 and 173. See sonnets: 'Spring', Hopkins (No. 45); 'The World is Too Much With Us', Wordsworth (No. 57); 'Shall I compare thee to a Summer's day', Shakespeare (No. 79); 'One day I wrote her name. . . .', Spenser (No. 80). For a modern sonnet, see 'High Flight', John Magee (No. 28).

stanza: Verse of a poem, which can be of various lengths such as a couplet (two lines) or quatrain (four lines) etc.

symbol: an object representing an idea or set value. *Example:* The daffodils symbolise the beauty and inspiration of nature to Wordsworth (No. 29).

tanka: Five-line poem of Japanese origin. See page 124.

theme: The general idea or concept communicated by a poem.

tone: Tone of voice, feelings, attitude of writer. See Mood, page 138.

verse: Stanza.

TEN CLASSROOM ACTIVITIES

While poetry, like music, can be enjoyed by the individual alone, it is not necessarily a solitary pastime appreciated only by intellectuals and the specially gifted. Just as with music, poetry too can be enjoyed by groups. For that reason many of the exercises which follow the poems involve group discussion and performance, whether in pairs, fours or larger groups.

Perhaps we need to give poetry a bit more space in our lives and classrooms. Can I suggest three things you need?

A. Personal Poetry Diary: Your own private property, not for criticism or examination, where you can write in a few favourite poems; the words of songs; memorable phrases you noticed or made up; photo-poetry, i.e. short descriptions which catch a scene or a character you noticed; your own poems etc.

B. Poetry Notice Board: Or a section of the class notice board where you can display poems or lyrics you like; the result of group activities; and poems written by members of the class.

C. Poetry Shelf: Where you keep a few poetry books or tapes for browsing or listening to in a free moment. See pages 141–4 for a list of suggestions. You may know of others you find interesting.

For audio material, See pages 145, 152, 158–9, 168–9, 173, 176, 180.

ACTIVITIES

1. **Find a poem you like**. Here the class activity consists of each student reading a poem of his/her choice. Say briefly why you chose it, why you like it – a sort of 'I like this because. . . .'. No fancy terms are necessary, just honest reaction. It works well if you sit around in a circle. You may need to agree ground rules such as 'Respect for other people's choices even if you think they're rubbish'. You can ask to hear a poem a second time.

2. **Illustrate a poem**. Find a picture to illustrate an image or catch the mood of a poem you like. Read the poem aloud and explain why you chose the illustration.

3. **Theme Day**. Most of the work for this is done beforehand by pairs or groups of four, searching out poems on a particular theme such as Breaking Out; Family; Big Moments; Decisions; The World Around Us; Animal Poems; People in the Environment etc. You may want to include the lyrics of songs as well as poems.

4. **The Poet is . . . The Singer is . . . .** Working in groups, prepare and introduce the work of a poet or singer.

5. **Listen to poetry tapes**, such as those recommended below or any others you know. Then, working in groups, tape your own poetry selection, with appropriate music.
   - 'Poems and Poems 2' – selected readings compiled by Michael Harrison and Christopher Stuart-Clark. Includes some modern poets readings their own work. Oxford University Press.
   - 'The Abbey Reads' series, featuring Irish writers and a selection from the old Intermediate Certificate courses.
   - 'A Child's Christmas in Wales', read by Dylan Thomas. Collins Audio Cassette.
   - 'Dylan Thomas Reading His Poetry'. Collins Audio Cassette.
   - 'The Poetry of Thomas Hardy' read by Richard Burton. Collins Audio Cassette.
   - 'Richard Burton – A Personal Anthology'. Argo Cassettes.

6. **Interview**. Interview a person about a favourite poem. A reading plus question and answer session to be taped and played back.

7. **Form Day**. Just as 'find a poem you like', except this time it is 'Find a Sonnet' or 'Find a Ballad' or whatever is the chosen form.

8. **Write and read your own poetry**. If you are going to write in class, then some background music may be helpful. Try:

   'White Winds', Andreas Vollenweider   'Ambient', Brian Eno
   'Legend', Clannad   'Oxygene', Jean Michael Jarre
   'Victorialand', The Cocteau Twins   'The Brendan Voyage', Shaun Davey
   or any mood music.

9. **Display or publish**. You can display the work of groups or works on a theme on the notice board. Re-write or hand-print work so that it displays well. If you have enough good material, then think of a class poetry broadsheet to be sold in the school.

10. **Invite a poet to visit your class.**

POETRY YOU WILL ENJOY

1. 'Young Words', Macmillan.
These award-winning entries for the 1987 W.H. Smith Young Writers' Competition make great reading. The stories and poems by students of all ages from 6 to 16 never fail to surprise and impress. Something to aim for.

2. 'Irish Schools Creative Writing Prudential Awards'.
This Irish equivalent of 'Words' is published annually. When you've read it you may like to enter one of the competitions.

3. 'Strictly Private', Roger McGough (ed.) Puffin Plus.
There are poems here to amuse you, sadden you, disgust you, delight you, open your eyes, make you think. Great variety and a lot of fun.

4. 'I Like This Poem', Kaye Webb (ed.). Puffin.
A collection of poems chosen by young people, from ages 6 to 15, with reasons for choice given in each case. Don't just stop at your own age group – it's always interesting to see why someone else likes a poem you know.

5. 'Salford Road and Other Poems', Gareth Owen. Collins Young Lions.
These poems of school and home life are very real and they also have a sense of humour.

6. 'So Far, So Good', Mick Gowar. Puffin Plus Poetry.
Poems about the ordinary yet important happenings of everyday life: going to the beach; learning the guitar; falling in love; pocket money; English class; drugs and sport etc.

7. 'New Angles', Books 1 and 2. John Foster (ed.). Oxford University Press.
Two volumes of contemporary poetry with great variety and well illustrated. You should find something to think and talk about here – poverty; education; tragedy; skinheads; nuclear power; breakdancing; advertising, to name but a very few.

8. Oxford University Press Series. Compiled by John Foster, 'A Third, a Fourth, a Fifth Poetry Book' etc.
It's great to find poems so well presented with full colour illustrations. Books to browse through.

9. 'Nine O'Clock Bell' chosen by Raymond Wilson, Viking Kestrel.
Obviously poems about school, but I'll bet you never imagined your school could provide so many topics worth writing about – 134 poems in all. Most aspects of the daily grind are explored with sympathy, humour and insight.

10. 'Irish Poems for Young People', Quinn and Cashman (ed.). Wolfhound Press.
You'll find poems on: animals; birds; beauty; childhood; dreams; humour; movement; mystery; places; history; nature; people and prayer. There's a huge variety of attitudes and styles here. You'll need an Irish poetry book on your shelf.

11. 'Spaceways', an anthology of space poems, John Foster (ed.). Oxford University Press.
12. 'Roger McGough – Selected Poems'. Jonathan Cape.
13. 'What on Earth', poems with a conservation theme. Judith Nicholls (eds.). Faber & Faber.
14. 'Every Man will Shout', an anthology of modern verse, compiled by Roger Mansfield. Isobel Armstrong (ed.). Oxford University Press.
15. 'Limerick Delight', chosen by O.E. Parrott. Puffin.
16. 'When Grandmama Fell Off the Boat', Harry Graham. Methuen.
17. 'Every Poem Tells a Story', chosen by Raymond Wilson. Viking Kestrel.
18. 'The Young Dragon Book of Verse', Michael Harrison and Christopher Stuart-Clark (ed.). Oxford University Press.
19. 'The New Dragon Book of Poetry', Harrison and Stuart-Clark (ed.). Oxford University Press.
20. 'The Windmill Book of Poetry', David Orme (ed.). Heinemann Educational.
21. 'Poems in Focus', Christopher Martin (ed.). Oxford University Press.
22. Series: A Puffin Quartet, Quintet and Sextet of Poets. Puffin.
23. 'Out and About', poems of the outdoors. Chosen by Raymond Wilson. Puffin.
24. 'In Time of War', Anne Harvey (ed.). Puffin Plus Poetry.
25. 'Narrative Poems', Michael Harrison and Christopher Stuart-Clark (ed.). Oxford University Press.
26. 'The Rattle Bag', Seamus Heaney & Ted Hughes (ed.). Faber & Faber.
27. 'Messages', compiled by Naomi Lewis. Faber & Faber.
28. 'A Flock of Words', David Macay (collected). The Bodley Head.
29. 'The Faber Book of 20th Century Women's Poetry'. Fleur Adcock (ed.).
30. 'Ted Hughes – Selected Poetry'. Faber & Faber

A BRIEF SELECTION OF IRISH POETS
(in alphabetical order)

'The Selected Paul Durcan', Edna Longley (ed.). Blackstaff Press.
'Not Common Speech', Davoren Hanna. Raven Arts Press.
'Seamus Heaney Selected Poems'. Faber & Faber.
'Welcome to my Head', Pat Ingoldsby. Rainbow.
'Collected Poems, Patrick Kavanagh'.
'A Time for Voices – Selected Poems 1960-1990', Brendan Kennelly. Bloodaxe Books.
'New Selected Poems', John Montague. Gallery Books.
'The Christy Moore Songbook', Frank Connolly (ed.). Brandon.

'Dam-burst of Dreams', Christopher Nolan. Weidenfeld and Nicholson.
'Taking My Pen for a Walk', Julie O'Callaghan. Orchard Books and Collins Teen Tracks.
'Poets from the North of Ireland', Frank Ormsby (ed.). Blackstaff Press.
'The Younger Irish Poets', Gerald Dawe (ed.). Blackstaff Press.

WRITING AND APPRECIATING POETRY

'Writing Poems', Michael Harrison and Christopher Stuart-Clark. Oxford University Press.
'Poetry 2 and Poetry 3', John F. Foster (ed.). Macmillan Education.
'Appreciating Poetry', Sadler, Hayllar and Powell. Macmillan.
'The Poetry Show 1, 2, and 3'. David Orme and James Sale. Macmillan Education.
'On Common Ground' – a programme for teaching poetry, Jill Pirrie. Hodder and Stoughton.

EXPLORING THE POEMS
WORDS & MUSIC ON THE THEMES

SECTION A – BREAKING OUT

Reading on the Theme: Novels
'Freaky Friday', Mary Rodgers
'The Freedom Machine', Joan Lingard
'The Great Gilly Hopkins', Katherine Paterson
'Huckleberry Finn', Mark Twain
'My Side of the Mountain', Jean George
'Torch', Jill Paton Walsh

Music Suggestions
'All us Boys', Toto
'Another Brick in the Wall, Part II', Pink Floyd
'Born to be Wild', The Cult
'Break up the Family', Morrissey
'Escape', Metallica
'Fool for Temptation', The 4 of Us
'Please Don't Treat me like a Child', Helen Shapiro
'Waterfall', The Stone Roses
'Wild Life', INXS

Exploring the Poems

'HAIRSTYLE', JOHN AGARD (NO. 1)
GROUP DISCUSSION
1. Have you ever had similar experiences about your hair or clothes? Talk about it.
2. Do you feel the same way about it as the poet feels? REPORT BACK.
THE POEM
3. The poet uses colourful images, in this case metaphors, to convey the extraordinary hairstyles. What type of hairstyle does each metaphor suggest to you? Do you think it is a good metaphor? Why?
4. What is the poet's attitude to the reader or onlooker? What phrases suggest this?
5. Write down one question you have about the poem.
DESCRIPTIVE WRITING
6. Study a photograph of a hairstyle or items of clothes currently in fashion and write three descriptive paragraphs about it. Use metaphors or other ideas to convey your thoughts.
MEDIA
7. Design an advertising poster for a hair salon or clothes shop. (You can just describe the poster if you don't wish to draw it.) Compose a slogan for it.
DEBATE
8. What are your school rules regarding hairstyle and dress? Have a debate on this or debate the motion: 'The apparel oft proclaims the man' (Shakespeare).

'RECKLESS', PETE BROWN (NO. 2)
DIALOGUE
1. Write a dialogue between a parent and a young person about 'teeth'.
MEDIA
2. Compose some slogans for the walls of a dentist's waiting room.

'CHILD ON TOP OF A GREENHOUSE', THEODORE ROETHKE (NO. 3)
DRAMA
1. Working in pairs, rehearse and perform a dialogue between any two characters watching this scene – such as father; mother; aunt; brother; sister; owner of the greenhouse etc.
THE POEM
2. In your own words, say what the poet is describing.
3. What words or phrases catch your attention? Why?

4. The poet uses two comparison images or similes. Can you find them? What do they suggest to you? What do they add to the atmosphere of the poem?

5. What do you think the poet wants you to feel? Give reasons.

DESCRIPTIVE WRITING

6. Can you remember climbing a tree or your first swim or any other dangerous and dramatic experience you had when you were younger? Try to remember the details – the kind of day it was; the colour or feel of the tree or water; what you noticed; how you felt at that moment. Use images to catch the scene. Write three paragraphs.

7. Can you convert this memory of your childhood experience into a poem?

'A SONG IN THE FRONT YARD', GWENDOLYN BROOKS (NO. 4)

THE POEM (for group discussion)

1. Read the poem quietly a number of times and then consider the following. Are these the thoughts of: (a) a young girl; or (b) could they apply to an older student? Talk about this and then list all the clues which would make you favour (a) and those which suggest (b). REPORT BACK.

2. Could the front yard and the back yard stand for something more than just the yards of a house? What do you suggest?

3. How does the speaker feel – angry; defiant; frustrated; other? What do you think she means when she says 'a girl gets sick of a rose'?

4. What words or phrases catch your attention? Why? REPORT BACK.

5. What do you think is the theme or general idea behind the poem? Write a paragraph on this.

DRAMA (for groups)

6. What can we say to the girl? Invent a short drama for voices. You might use an empty chair to represent the girl, with group members taking up roles as mother/father; older brother/sister; friend of her own age; boy/girl from where the 'charity children' play etc.

CREATIVE WRITING

7. Write a piece beginning with one of the following:

   'I've stayed in school all my life . . .'
   'I've been well behaved all my life . . .'
   'I've been difficult all my life . . .'
   'I've been in the A class all my life . . .'
   'I've driven in the slow lane all my life . . .'

READING

8. Read the poem 'My Parents kept me from Children who were Rough', by Stephen Spender.

   You might enjoy '8 + 1', a collection of short stories by Robert Cormier.

'THE BOYS OF WINTER', ALAN BOLD (NO. 5)
MEDIA
1. You are the director of a film crew making a poetry video and you want scenes to accompany the sound track of this poem. Your film must be true to the poem. Write your filming instructions in Chart A (page 149). Study Chart B (pages 150–151) for information on a range of shots.
DRAMA (for groups or rows)
2. A row or rows might take up roles as people in a queue at the corner of Princes Street. Decide who and what you are and why exactly you are there. What thoughts are going through your mind as you watch these boys? Think about it. Then each student speaks in turn, to form a collage of the inner thoughts of the people in the queue.
3. If there are differing views, then perhaps a discussion or argument might develop.
4. Other students might like to do the inner voices of the Boys of Winter.
5. Another row can be yourselves. What can you say to these boys? Talk to them.
6. What slogans do you think they wrote?
THE POEM
7. What images or pictures from the poem do you notice most and why?
8. Did you notice the rhyming scheme? What effect does the rhyme have?
WRITING
9. Write a short essay on 'Teenage Unemployment'.

'WARNING', JENNY JOSEPH (NO. 6)
THE POEM
1. Who is the speaker in this poem: an old woman; a middle-aged parent; a young girl? Explain.
2. A lot of humour in this poem is created by the contrast between what we would expect of the speaker and what she actually says. This technique is called IRONY and is often used to show up contradictions. What contrasts do you like best and why?
3. From your reading of what the poet wishes to do when she 'breaks out', what could we infer about the kind of person she is now? Write three paragraphs about her.
4. What is the poet trying to say here? What is the theme? Write a paragraph about it.
CREATIVE WRITING
5. Write a poem beginning: 'When I am a 5th year . . . '

Chart A

Shot No.	Lines/Phrases	Type of shot	Description of Scene as you see it. Ideas for sound effects, music etc.
1	'Snow around their boots, they gather like an embodiment of the weather'	C.U.	C.U. of Doc Martens stomping threateningly in the snow
2			
3			
4			
5 etc.			

*In your groups, explain the reasons for your choice of shots.

Chart B   **Some Shots**

L.S. = Long Shot
(shows the whole scene)

M.S. = Medium Shot
(an in-between shot which shows several people, close enough so that we can see their expressions, gestures etc.)

C.U. = Close-up
(shows part of the body such as hands or feet but most often shows the face)

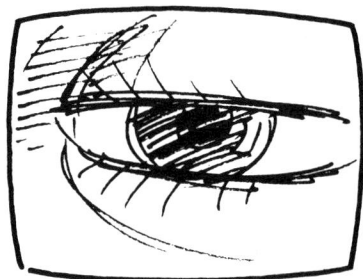

E.C.U. = Extreme Close-up
(shows mouth or eye or nose etc.)

H.A. = High Angle
(picture taken from above, often suggests subject is small or in danger)

L.A. = Low Angle
(Camera is looking up at the subject making him or her appear bigger or threatening etc.)

Chart B *continued*

Moving Shots or Changing Shots

Pan: Move camera in wide circular sweep around a great part of the scene

Track: Keep camera moving parallel to a moving object

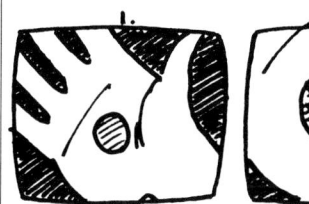

Zoom: Camera can move in to show a detail of the scene or it can zoom out

Cut: Direct change from one picture to the next

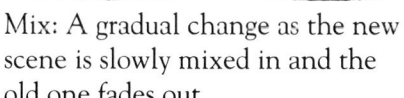

Mix: A gradual change as the new scene is slowly mixed in and the old one fades out

Fade: Fade in – the gradual appearance of a picture. Fade out – picture fades out to a black colour

'SHE'S LEAVING HOME', JOHN LENNON AND PAUL McCARTNEY (NO. 7)

THE LYRICS
1. The lyrics in this song are spoken or sung by different voices. Who is speaking where?
2. What image catches your attention most? Why?
3. What do you think is the effect created by all the long vowel sounds in 'She's leaving . . .', etc.

WRITING
4. Write your version of the note that she left.

DRAMA
5. In groups of three, improvise the dialogue that might have occurred before this event. Then write it down and play it to the class.

SONG LYRICS
6. Each group might introduce a song or songs it likes and/or play a tape of it to the class. You might also introduce the work of a singer you appreciate and play a selection of their songs in class. An introduction might include: the themes or issues he or she likes to write about; what you like about the lyrics and music; any information you have on the singer's life and work etc.

'GROWING UP?' WES MAGEE (NO. 8)

1. Is this poem like your own experience in any way? How?
2. What view of himself do you think Wes Magee has in this poem? What lines suggest it?
3. Read 'Freaky Friday', a short novel by Mary Rodgers, about a girl who turns into her mother and suddenly gets a very different view of teenagers! Great fun.

SECTION B – FAMILY

Reading on the Theme: Novels

'Buddy', Nigel Hinton
'My Family and Other Animals', Gerald Durrell
'The Gooseberry', Joan Lingard
'No Place Like', Gene Kemp
'Over the Water', Maude Casey
'Welcome Home, Jellybean', Marlene Fanta Shyer

Poems

'A Prayer for my Daughter', W.B. Yeats
'Father and Son', F.R. Higgins
'Golden Stockings', Oliver St John Gogarty
'In Memory of my Mother', Patrick Kavanagh
'Memory of my Father', Patrick Kavanagh

Music Suggestions

'Father to Son', Phil Collins
'Let's Stick Together', Bryan Ferry
'My Old Man', The Fureys/Phil Coulter
Can you think of others?

Exploring the Poems

'THE PARENT', OGDEN NASH (NO. 9)
Can you attempt a two-line rhyme (couplet) about any member of your family?

'MY SISTER BETTY', GARETH OWEN (NO. 10)
THE POEM

> **1.** The humour in this poem depends largely on the use of CARICATURE – where a picture or description of someone is exaggerated in order to appear ridiculous.

How is the picture of the actress caricatured here? Write three paragraphs on this.

> **2.** Humour is also achieved through the use of IRONY – which means: (a) a slightly sarcastic use of words to mean the opposite of what is said; and (b) an occurrence which is the opposite of that expected.

Can you find examples of both kinds of irony here?

CREATIVE WRITING
3. Compose a piece of caricature on your young brother who thinks he'll play for Ireland in the World Cup!

'HUGGER MUGGER', KIT WRIGHT (NO. 11)
CREATIVE WRITING
Write an account of an embarrassing incident, real or imaginary, which happened to you.

POEMS BY HARRY GRAHAM (NOS. 12-16)
THE POEMS

> A SATIRE is the word used to describe any work in which vice, nastiness, foolishness or a foolish person is held up to ridicule. The tone of a satire, while being humourous, can also be quite bitter and cutting. You'll notice that there is a much more vicious or cutting tone in the Harry Graham verses than in 'My Sister Betty'.

1. Can you say who is being satirised in each verse and how?
2. You'll notice that the lines rhyme in pairs. These are called *rhyming couplets*. Do you think this helps the satire? Explain.

'TO MY MOTHER', GEORGE BARKER (NO. 17)

(**Note:** Rabelais – sixteenth century French writer, renowned for his gross sense of humour and exuberant language.)

THE POEM

Good poetry sometimes implies or suggests a good deal more than it actually says.
1. In two separate columns, list: (a) what George Barker actually states about his mother; and (b) what he implies. Quote the phrases or line to support what you say in each case.
2. In particular, what do the similes used suggest about her?
3. What feelings does the poet have for his mother and what lines suggest this most strongly?
4. What does the last line mean for you?
5. Look at some Mother's Day or Father's Day cards and examine the greetings. Which seems more true? Why?

'MOTHER OF THE GROOM', SEAMUS HEANEY (NO. 18)

MEDIA (for individual work)
1. Using the technique described on pages 148–150, draw up a chart of filming instructions for the shooting of a video to accompany this poem.
2. (for groups) Explain and discuss your work.

THE POEM
3. What images appeal to you most and why? Write three paragraphs on this.
4. Can you express what you think is the theme of the poem, in one paragraph? Could you do it in one sentence and be satisfied that you had caught the main idea?
5. What do you think the poet wants you to feel? Explain why you say this.

'DIGGING', SEAMUS HEANEY (NO. 19)

THE POEM (for individuals or group discussion)
1. Leaving out the first and last stanzas for the moment, what is the poet describing in the rest of the poem?
2. What pictures can you see most clearly? Are the pictures or images very detailed? What details stick in your mind? Explain.
3. As well as sight images, the poet also uses touch images in order to fill out the picture for us. How many of these can you find?
4. There are also many sounds in this poem.

> When the sound of the word is similar to the meaning, it is called ONOMATOPOEIA. For example: 'a clean rasping sound'— the *ra* sound of rasping is rough and harsh, just like the meaning of the word.

Can you find any other onomatopoeic words in the poem? REPORT BACK.

5. Now look at the whole poem again. The poet makes a comparison between his own work and that of his father. When the comparison runs the whole length of the poem, it is called an EXTENDED METAPHOR. Can you explain this one? What points of comparison are there between Seamus Heaney's work and that of this father?
DESCRIPTIVE WRITING
6. Write 5 paragraphs on one of the following: a person cutting a hedge; sowing potatoes; harvesting corn; weeding the garden; washing up; painting a wall; or any activity you have observed closely. Use images from the different senses – sight, sound, touch, smell and taste – where appropriate.
7. Can you convert your description into a metaphor poem?

'THE CAGE', JOHN MONTAGUE (NO. 20)
(**Note:** *Odysseus* – Greek legendary hero of the epic poem, 'The Odyssey', by Homer. He survived the Trojan War but, on his return, sea storms drove him around the oceans and kept him from home for ten years. *Telemachus* – the son of Odysseus and Penelope, in the 'Odyssey'.)
DISCUSSION (for groups)
What points of comparison and contrast can you find between this poem and 'Digging'? Discuss and draw up a list, giving examples of each point.
PROJECTS
A. For Groups
Working on the theme of family or relations, find poems you like for a poetry reading or for a wall display. Be prepared to introduce your poem to the class. Here are some you may enjoy.
   'Sad Aunt Madge', Roger McGough
   'Grandfather', Derek Mahon
   'Memory of My Father', Patrick Kavanagh
   'In Memory of my Mother', Patrick Kavanagh
   'My Father', Ted Hughes
   'Gloria, My Little Sister', Russell Hoban
   'My Papa's Waltz', Theodore Roethke

B. Creative Writing
Write a poem about a grandmother or grandfather, or any family member or any person you have observed closely.
- First, spend some time thinking about that person and jot down the details as you remember them.
- What images or pictures do the details suggest in your mind?
- Work your ideas into a poem. Rewrite and reshape until it pleases you and you are happy that it says exactly what you want it to say.

SECTION C – DECISIONS/CHOICES

Exploring The Poems

'TICH MILLER', WENDY COPE (NO. 21)
CONSIDER
1. Do you have any experience of the situation described in this poem?
MIME (for groups of 5)
2. First read the poem silently, a number of times. Each student should then read it to the group. The others can then question the reader as to why he/she read certain lines in that way. Then agree on one reader who will do the group reading.

The other group members should then devise a mime to accompany the reading. This mime should help the audience to appreciate the poem better. It can be a mime of a number of images from the poem (it won't work if you try to mine everything) or an abstract mime which would create the mood. Each group then performs in turn. Finish with a *class round* on the poem, i.e. each student gets to make one statement beginning (this time) 'I noticed that . . .'.
WRITING
3. Write a diary entry as you imagine Tich Miller might have written it.
4. Write a diary entry as one of the team captains might have written it.
5. Write a letter to the school principal as Tich Miller's mother or father might have written it.

'TRUTH', BARRIE WADE (NO. 22)
Read the poem and think about it. You might memorise it.

'HERO', MICK GOWAR (NO. 23)
DRAMA ROUND
1. When you have read the poem silently a number of times, each student addresses the hero with one statement beginning: 'Well, hero . . .'.
2. Working in pairs, rehearse a conversation between the hero and his visitor. One student could read the hero's part and the other could intersperse a new dialogue. Write it and then perform it.
DEBATE
3. Working in groups, consider and submit titles for three debates which stem from the issues aired in this poem. Then debate them.
THE POEM
4. Comment on the title of the poem.

'LIMBO', D.M. THOMAS (NO. 24)
DRAMA LEAD-IN (N.B. *BEFORE* READING THE POEM)
1. For groups of 7. You are in a life raft, seemingly the only survivors of a major disaster. Each student chooses a role: doctor, teacher, architect, politician etc. The raft can only hold 6 in safety. Each must argue his or her need to stay aboard. REPORT BACK on the outcome.
THE POEM
2. Read the poem and think about it. What are your reactions to it? What did you like and dislike about it?
3. In a brief paragraph, say what the theme is. Can you put it in one sentence?
CREATIVE WRITING
4. Write the diary of Zoe for the week in which the incident occurred.

'EDIBLE ANECDOTE NO 24', JULIE O'CALLAGHAN (NO. 25)
Working in groups of 3, rehearse and perform this as a dialogue with commentary. Discuss each group's interpretation of the text.

'THE CHOOSING', LIZ LOCHHEAD (NO. 26)
THE POEM
1. What is the poet trying to describe here?
2. What do you think is important about the poem?
3. What images do you think are effective and why?
4. Is the title ironic? Explain.

'HIGH FLIGHT', JOHN MAGEE (NO. 27)
THE POEM
1. What experience is the poet describing here?
2. What does the poet feel about the experience? What words or phrases carry the feeling?
3. What images catch your attention? How important are adjectives in creating these images?
4. How is the sense of power and energy conveyed? Study the verbs.
5. If we call the rhyme at the end of the first line *a* and that at the end of the second *b* and so on, can you work out the rhyming scheme?
6. What is a sonnet? (See page 164.)

'THE ROAD NOT TAKEN', ROBERT FROST (NO. 28)
THE POEM
1. Read this poem carefully a number of times and then do a class round on it. But this time, each statement must be in the form of a question: example 'Where is he coming from?' or . . .

2. Discuss the poem in your small groups and decide on the best way of presenting it to the class.
3. Can you find out anything about Robert Frost? REPORT BACK.
PROJECT
4. Do you know any poems, stories or novels which deal with dramatic decisions? Introduce one to the class. Have you read 'The Guilty Party' by Joan Lingard?
5. Do you have any suggestions for music dealing with decisions/choices? Example: 'At Seventeen', Janis Ian; 'Hot Dogs and Hamburgers', John Cougar Mellancamp; 'The Ordinary Boys', Morrissey. Introduce a piece of music on this theme.

SECTION D – THE WORLD AROUND US... AND BEYOND

Reading on the Theme: Novels
'The Heart of the Valley', Nigel Hinton
'The Midnight Fox', Betsy Byars
'The Red Pony', John Steinbeck
'Watership Down', Richard Adams
'Z for Zachariah', Robert C. O'Brien

Non-fiction
'To the Waters and the Wild', Gerrit Van Gelderen

Other Poems
'Binsey Poplars', Gerard Manley Hopkins
'The Darkling Thrush', Thomas Hardy
'The Eagle', Alfred, Lord Tennyson
'The Hope of Wings', Brendan Kennelly
'Inversnaid', Gerard Manley Hopkins
'Spraying the Potatoes', Patrick Kavanagh
'To the Man after the Harrow', Patrick Kavanagh
'What on Earth', poems with a conservation theme, Judith Nichols (Ed.). Faber & Faber

Music Suggestions
Classical/Instruments/Natural Sound:
'The Brendan Voyage', Shaun Davey
'Carnival of the Animals', Saint Saens
'La Mer', Debussy
'Boireann', (the Burren), John Buckley
'The Four Seasons', Vivaldi

'Entrance to the Secret Lagoon', New World Cassettes
'The Lark Ascending', Vaughan Williams
'New Grange', Clannad
'The Pastoral Symphony', Beethoven
'Rain Forest Requiem', a day in the life of the Amazon rain forest, Mankind Music and British Library National Sound Archive.
'Reverence', whale songs, interspersed with flute music. Terry Oldfield, New World Cassettes
'Restful Sounds', sounds of the seashore, sounds of the countryside. New World Cassettes
'Sea Pictures', Elgar
'Song of the Sea Shore', James Galway
'The Trout', Schubert

Vocals
'Autumn Leaves', Nat King Cole
'Bright Eyes', 'Watership Down' soundtrack
'Born Free', Don Black & John Barry
Songs from 'Cats', Andrew Lloyd Weber
'October', U2
'Ol' Man River', Paul Robeson
'Poisoning Pigeons in the Park', Tom Lehrer

And Beyond:
'E.T.' the soundtrack
'The Planets', Gustav Holst
'A Spaceman Came Travelling', Chris de Burgh
'Space Oddity', David Bowie
'Thin Halo of Blue', RTE entry for the 1990 Prix d'Italia, John Buckley
'2001 – A Space Odyssey', the soundtrack

Exploring the Poems

'I WANDERED LONELY AS A CLOUD', WILLIAM WORDSWORTH (NO. 29)
THE POEM
1. What was the poet's state of mind before he saw the display of daffodils? Be serious! What image does he use to suggest this? Do you think it is an effective one?
2. How was the poet's mood altered? Where is this suggested?
3. What deeper significance did the scene have for Wordsworth? Have the daffodils become a symbol of something for him? Comment.
4. What do you think is meant by the 'inward eye'?

5. Could an experience like this happen to you or anyone? Write about it.
PROJECT
6. Produce a wall chart on the life and works of William Wordsworth.

'PIED BEAUTY', GERARD MANLEY HOPKINS (NO. 30)
Notes:
Pied – mixed colours
Dappled – spotted or shaded in colour
Brinded – from brindled, i.e. tawny brown, streaked with another colour
In stipple – painted in dots
Fresh-firecoal chestnut-falls – fallen chestnuts the colour of coals of fire
Plotted and Pieced – the pattern and design of the fields
Fold – an enclosure for sheep
Fallow – land that is ploughed but not sown for a year
Plough – ploughed land
All Trades – people of different occupations
Counter – contrasting
Fathers-forth – creates

THE POEM
1. Hopkins is pointing out what great variety there is in nature and in the world. The poem is constructed as a hymn of praise to God who created all this variety. What are the things Hopkins lists as interesting examples of this variety?
2. What examples appeal to you most? Why?
3. Does he go out of his way to describe these in an unusual and interesting way? Explain.
4. For poetic and musical effect he uses ALLITERATION in his descriptions. *Example*: 'skies of couple colour'. List any other examples of alliteration you can find.
WRITING
5. Using your own preferences for examples of variety in the world, write a poem beginning 'Glory be to God for dappled things . . .'.

'PARROT', ALAN BROWNJOHN (NO. 31)
Read the short story 'Tobermory' by Saki.

'PIGEONS', RICHARD KELL (NO. 32)
BEFORE you read the poem:
1. Write the word 'Pigeons' on a blank page. Think about how they look, move, behave, fly etc. – everything you can remember about them. Think about sounds, colours, texture etc. Jot down all your observations *in brief phrases*.

THE POEM
2. Now read the poem a number of times. Does Richard Kell describe any aspect of pigeons which you had noticed? Does he capture that aspect well? Explain.
3. Now look again at all the other images he uses. They are mostly similes or metaphors, comparing pigeons with people or activities. What do you think of each one? Write a paragraph on each. Are they all sight images? Explain.
4. Study the verbs the poet uses to capture the activities. Write two paragraphs on them.
DESCRIPTIVE WRITING
5. Study any other bird, wild or captive, and write five paragraphs or a poem about it. You might first jot down lots of ideas *in brief phrases* and then pick the images which seem most true to the bird and build a poem around them.

'THE BATTERY HEN', PAM AYRES (NO. 33)
GROUPS
1. What does Pam Ayres want us to feel here? Discuss and explain your opinions.
2. Is this poetry? REPORT BACK.

'SAINT FRANCIS AND THE BIRDS', SEAMUS HEANEY (NO. 34)
THE POEM
1. What is the poet describing here? Do you think he does it well? Explain.
2. Can you put the theme of this poem in a paragraph or, better still, in a sentence? Revise until you are happy with your answer.

'THE DOG LOVERS', SPIKE MILLIGAN (NO. 35)
'DOG EXERCISING MAN', KEITH BOSLEY (NO. 36)
What similarities and differences can you find between these two poems?
Think of: theme; speaker and point of view; tone – serious, critical, humourous, ironic etc; imagery; diction (choice of words) etc.

'TIME FOR THE KNIFE', BRENDAN KENNELLY (NO. 37)
THE POEM
1. When you have read this poem a number of times, don't talk about it, just sit and think. Now jot down your first reactions. If you wish, you can then share them with your group or the class.
2. The graphic details are an important part of this poem. What details catch your attention most forcefully? Why?
3. Is Enright a cruel man? Consider: . . . *caressing the brown and white head* . . . *the penknife* . . . *flicked open* . . . *pitched it into the grass*. What do you think is Enright's attitude to the operation?

4. The pup's suffering is described in three similes. Write a paragraph on each of them.

5. Read 'The Early Purges' by Seamus Heaney.

'DIARY OF A CHURCH MOUSE', JOHN BETJEMAN (NO. 38)

Notes:

Cassock – long, black tunic worn by the clergy

Hassock – cushion for kneeling

Baize – woollen green cloth used for covering or to insulate the back of a door

Whitsun – 7th Sunday after Easter, commemorating the descent of the Holy Spirit at Pentecost

Harvest Festival – Thanksgiving service for the harvest, at which the church is decorated with fruit, grain and other harvest fare.

Evensong – Evening prayer in the Church of England

High Church – A section of the Church of England which attaches great importance to the sights, sounds, ceremonial and rituals of worship; also to bishops, priests, sacraments etc.

Low Church – That section of the Church of England which gives only low place to the aforementioned and concentrates more on scripture as the centre of worship.

THE POEM

1. This poem changes from being straight-forwardly descriptive in the early stanzas to being gently satirical. Who or what is the poet criticising?

2. Do you think the poet's use of rhyming couplets helps the satire?

3. Explain the irony in the passage beginning 'Within the human world I know . . .'.

'SHEEP', TED HUGHES (NO. 39)

THE POEM

1. What is the poet describing here?

2. What does the poet want us to feel? Write a note about the tone of this poem, using examples of words and phrases to prove your point of view.

3. What images catch your attention? Explain your reaction to these images.

'THE FOX', ADRIAN MITCHELL (NO. 40)

BEFORE you read the poem:

1. Spend time thinking about 'The Difficult Life of the Fox'. Using single words or short phrases, jot down any ideas you have.

2. Did you think in the 1st person or the 3rd person? Did you think *as* the fox or *about* the fox? Which is the better approach to the subject?

GROUP DISCUSSION
3. Now read the poem a number of times and consider in your groups:
(a) What is the dilemma the fox faces?
(b) What is his attitude to tame animals?
(c) What are his feelings about his life?
(d) Are all his memories gloomy?
(e) What is his attitude towards the future?
Find phrases or lines to back up your answers. REPORT BACK.
THE POEM
4. The fox is hemmed in on one side by the town life which he distrusts and on the other by the weather which he fears. Sometimes he describes the weather, the elements, the seasons, as if they were live enemies. What is the effect of this?
5. Can you work out the rhyming scheme for this poem?

'THE TYGER', WILLIAM BLAKE (NO. 41)
THE POEM
1. This is not just a simple description of a tiger. What exactly is the poet describing here?
2. What aspects of the tiger does the poet want to emphasise in each of the first four verses?
3. The word 'symmetry' here probably refers to the beauty of a well-structured and proportioned body. Do you think 'fearful' is an unusual adjective to use with it? Look up the meaning of the word 'paradox'. Is it an appropriate devise here?
4. The poem is as much about the nature of God who created the tiger as it is about the animal. What picture of God emerges? Look at each of the verses in turn.
5. Write two paragraphs on the theme of this poem.

'FOG', CARL SANDBURG (NO. 42)
THE POEM
1. Explain the comparison or metaphor which the poet uses to describe the fog. Do you think it is appropriate?
CREATIVE WRITING
2. Write a metaphor poem on one of the following: rain; snow; wind; moonlight; the tides; clouds.

'ROGUE LEAF', DEREK MAHON (NO. 43)
CREATIVE WRITING
Write a poem on the first flower of spring or the last apple of autumn.

'MARCH', PATRICK KAVANAGH (NO. 44)
What questions have you got about this poem?

'SPRING', GERARD MANLEY HOPKINS (NO. 45)
THE POEM

> The poem is a SONNET, written in the Italian or Petrarchan form. It has the usual 14 lines of a sonnet, but is divided in two sections: an *octave* – the first eight lines, and a *sestet* – the final 6. Usually we find a different idea or a change of tone in the sestet.

1. In the octave, what is the key phrase from which everything else follows?
2. In the sestet, to what does he compare spring?
3. What examples of the presence of spring does the poet highlight in the octave? Are they surprising or expected?
4. He uses alliteration to create musical effect. Underline the sequences.
5. He also uses words for their sound effects. Notice the onomatopoeia of 'lush' and 'wring'.
What does the texture of these words suggest? Can you find other onomatopoeic words?
6. To get across the feeling of energy and excitement, Hopkins sometimes runs one line into the next so that you need to read a number of lines without pausing. This is called ENJAMBMENT. See lines 3, 4, and 5. Can you find other examples?
7. In your own words, what exactly is Hopkins saying in the sestet?
8. Can you now write two paragraphs on the main themes of the poem?
9. Read the poem aloud and enjoy the sounds of the words.

'TO AUTUMN', JOHN KEATS (NO. 46)
Notes:

Barred Clouds – patterned in bars
Bloom – give a glow to
Bourn – small stream
Croft – small agricultural holding worked by a peasant
Gourd – large fleshy fruit
Sallows – low growing willow trees
Swath – a ridge of hay or corn which has just been cut
Winnowing – separating the grain from the chaff or covering at harvest time.

> The ODE: The ode originated in Classical Greece, where it was a poem meant to be sung. Modern odes are rhymed lyric poems. Odes are more public sounding than other lyrics and often deal with philosophical issues such as justice, truth, solitude, immortality, art etc. They tend to be solemn and stately in language and rhythm.

THE POEM
1. What general feeling about autumn do you get from the first stanza?
2. What do you think is the key statement in the first stanza?
3. All the images in the first stanza are of ripeness and fruitfulness. Which one do you prefer and why?
4. To which sense (sight, hearing, smell, taste, touch) do the images in the first stanza mainly refer?
5. Autumn is described as a person in stanza two. What personality traits does Keats give to autumn? Quote to support you views.
6. What senses are appealed to in this stanza? Give examples.
7. What atmosphere is created by the sounds of the words in the last line of stanza two? Explain.
8. The poet deals with the music of autumn in the third stanza. What do you think of the examples he chooses? Study his use of onomatopoeia to get across the sounds.
9. What season of the year is not referred to? Why?
10. Can you work out the rhyming scheme of the stanzas?

'WINTER' L.A.G. STRONG (NO. 47)
CREATIVE WRITING
Think about the comparison (simile) created in this poem. Try a simile poem on autumn or another season of the year.

'STOPPING BY WOODS ON A SNOWY EVENING', ROBERT FROST (NO. 48)
1. What do you like about this poem?
2. Read 'The Way Through the Woods', a poem by Rudyard Kipling.

'THE WOOD', DEREK MAHON (NO. 49)
1. Find another poem about trees which appeals to you and present it to the class.
2. Read: 'Binsey Poplars (felled 1879)' by Gerard Manley Hopkins; 'Throwing a Tree' by Thomas Hardy; 'Loveliest of Trees' by A.E. Houseman.

'THE SHELL', JAMES STEPHENS (NO. 50)
CREATIVE WRITING
1. Read the poem silently a number of times. Don't talk at all.
2. Play some appropriate background music such as 'Ambient 4' by Brian Eno, or 'White Winds' by Andreas Vollenweider and just *write*. You can write a poem or a story or a piece of descriptive prose or a letter etc. on whatever ideas are sparked off by the poem.
3. Share your writing with your group or the class.
4. If you feel you have to, you can then analyse the poem.

'THE TROUT', JOHN MONTAGUE (NO. 51)
THE POEM
1. This is a very quiet poem and yet electric with drama. Examine how the drama is built up.
2. Where would you locate the climax?
3. What do you like about this poem?

'THE SONG OF THE WHALE', KIT WRIGHT (NO. 52)
THE POEM
1. Did you notice the repetition in this song? Did you notice the contrast set up by the refrain?
2. Comment on the opening metaphor.
CREATIVE WRITING
3. The opening metaphor is very like a KENNING used in Anglo-Saxon poetry. This is a comparison image which was meant to capture the shape, movement and texture of the object. *Example*: The sea was described as 'the whale's road'; The wind as 'howl of the dying wolf'. Can you make kennings for some of the following: fisherman, sun, shark, volcano, jet plane.
4. Compose a protest song about any other environmental issue.
PROJECT
5. Have a Poetry Day entitled: 'Look around you'. Consider readings, music sessions etc. on the theme. You can find and present environmental poems or write and read your own.

'THE RIVER GOD', STEVIE SMITH (NO. 53)
THE POEM
1. Based on the evidence in the poem, compose a character sketch of the River God.
2. The river is described as if it were human. This is called PATHETIC FALLACY. What are the advantages of writing the poem in this way?
WRITING
3. Draft and write some rules on Water Safety.
4. Compose the song of the Mountain Stream, or the song of the Great Oak or that of the Forest God.

'THE DIVINER', SEAMUS HEANEY (NO. 54)
MEDIA
1. (for individuals) When you have read this poem a number of times, draw up a film director's chart, as on pages 149–151. Plan the shots you would use to accompany the reading of this poem. Try to be true to the mood of the poem.

2. (groups of 4) First discuss the poem – is everyone clear on what the poem is about? Each in turn should briefly explain his/her understanding of the piece.
3. Each group member now explains his or her film plot. Discuss the best interpretations of the poem. Revise your film plot if you now have a better idea for any shot. Choose one film plot for REPORT BACK to the class.
THE POEM
4. In one paragraph, explain the theme of the poem.
5. Write three paragraphs on your reaction to the poem.

'LIKE DOLMENS ROUND MY CHILDHOOD, THE OLD PEOPLE', JOHN MONTAGUE (NO. 55)
THE POEM
1. The world around us features the people we know, 'the characters' we encounter, as well as the natural flora and fauna. Which of John Montague's 'characters' do you find most interesting to think about? Why?
2. Do you think the simile of the title is appropriate? Why?
3. Compose a piece about a character you know or have read about. Write in paragraphs or stanzas.
4. Write an essay on 'The people who have influenced me' or 'My view of Ireland today'.
INTERVIEW HOMEWORK
5. Working in pairs, interview older people about their recollections of characters they knew or people who influenced them. Prepare the questions well in advance. Ask open-ended questions which will allow people to talk on. Record interviews in a notebook or on tape. REPORT BACK.
6. Can you find the words and music of 'The Sash' or 'The Auld Orange Flute'?

'AT THE BOMB TESTING SITE', WILLIAM STAFFORD (NO. 56)
THE POEM
1. What is the poet describing here?
2. What image catches your attention? Why?
3. What does the poet want us to feel? Explain.
4. Is this a tense or dramatic poem? Explain your view.
CREATIVE WRITING
5. Write a piece, through the eye of a creature, viewing any important moment in history. You can write in paragraphs or stanzas.
DEBATE
6. 'That nuclear power is the way forward for the 21st Century' or debate any aspect of the pros and cons of nuclear power.

'THE WORLD IS TOO MUCH WITH US', WILLIAM WORDSWORTH (NO. 57)

Notes:
> *Proteus* – in Greek legend, a sea-god who herded seals and could change his shape to avoid being questioned.
>
> *Triton* – in Greek legend, a merman, son of Poseidon, god of the sea and Amphitrite.

THE POEM (for group work)

1. In this sonnet, where exactly is the division between octave and sestet?
2. Discuss your understanding of what Wordsworth is saying in the octave.
3. Is there a new idea in the sestet? Discuss your understanding of what he is saying here. REPORT BACK.
4. Do you think Wordsworth has a point? Is it valid for today? Consider the phrases: 'Getting and spending, we lay waste our powers' . . . 'Little we see in nature that is ours' . . . 'For this, for everything, we are out of tune'. Prepare and deliver a two-minute speech on any of these phrases.

NOS 58-63 (INCLUSIVE)

PROJECT

Organise a Science Fiction Day for your class. Each student must introduce a science fiction story or poem or novel or writer to the class. (If you haven't got a favourite, then write one.) The introduction can be simple: information about the work and why you like it. Groups can then put the material together in the form of wall charts for display. Can you get a science fiction author to visit?

CREATIVE WRITING

1. Write a story about a space adventure.
2. Write an essay on: 'The Glories of Human Achievement'.

DESCRIPTIVE WRITING (groups)

3. Write explanatory descriptions of institutions, customs, scenes and other elements of our society to provide a guide for an extra-terrestrial. Put them into guide book form.

SECTION E – LOVE

A Medley of Music Suggestions

'At Seventeen', Janis Ian
'All I Want is You', U2
'All You Need is Love', The Beatles
'Anachy Gordon', Mary Black

'Barbara Allen', Art Gartfunkel
'Blue Sunday', The Doors
'Bunclody', (traditional)
'Can't Buy me Love', The Beatles

'Catch', The Cure
'Come Dancing', The Kinks
'Don't Wanna Loose You', Gloria Estefan
'Dreams of an Everyday Housewife', Ray Steevens
'I will Survive', Gloria Gaynor
'Lady in Red', Chris de Burgh
'Maria', from Westside Story
'Marry a Woman Uglier Than You', The Kings Singers
'Nancy Spain', sung by Christy Moore
'Never Tear Us Apart', INXS
'Peggy Gordon', (traditional)
'Raglan Road', written by Patrick Kavanagh
'Romeo's On Fire', The Stunning
'Sweet Thames Flow Softly', Ewan McColl
'Two Hearts', Phil Collins
'Úr Chnoc Chéin Mhic Cáinte', poem by Peadar O'Doirnín, set to music by Albert Fry
'The Whistling Gypsy', (traditional)
'Windmills of your Mind', Elaine Page
'Woman', John Lennon

Exploring The Poems

'KING OF THE KURZEL', MICK GOWAR (NO. 64)
THE POEM
1. What is the poet attempting to describe here?
2. What does he want the reader to feel? What lines show this best?
3. How is the boy's excitement communicated in the first stanza?
4. Is the feeling of awkwardness communicated well through the images used in the second stanza? Explain.
5. What do you think is meant by the last three lines of the third stanza?
6. Comment on the phrase 'appeared by chance' in the fourth stanza.
7. Comment on the final simile of the poem.
8. What is the effect of the short lines and the lack of punctuation in this poem? Read it aloud to yourself.
CREATIVE WRITING
9. Study a photograph of a couple and write a poem about their feelings. (See page 57.)
10. Describe an experience when you felt very inadequate or when you felt very happy.

'GIRL'S SONG', WILFRID GIBSON (NO. 65)
Read the poem and think about it.

'HE WISHES FOR THE CLOTHS OF HEAVEN', W.B. YEATS (NO. 66)
THE POEM
1. What are the poet's feelings here? Refer to lines.
2. The poet uses two metaphors here. What are they? Explain how he manages to mix one into the other.
CREATIVE WRITING
3. Write an essay entitled: 'Tread softly because you tread on my dreams'.

'FIRST KISS', ADAM PRITCHARD (NO. 67)
'No Soul?' – Comment.

'SONG FOR A BEAUTIFUL GIRL PETROL-PUMP ATTENDANT ON THE MOTORWAY', ADRIAN HENRI (NO. 68)
'Poor Lad!' – Comment.

'THE PASSIONATE SHEPHERD TO HIS LOVE', CHRISTOPHER MARLOWE (NO. 69)
Notes:
>   *Prove* (1.2) – experience
>   *Dales* (1.3) – valleys
>   *Madrigals* (2.4) – song for several voices in harmony
>   *Posies/poesy* (3.2) – small bunches of sweet scented flowers
>   *Kirtle* (3.3) – robe
>   *Swain* (6.1) – young countryman

THE POEM
1. What is the tone or mood of this poem? Write three paragraphs on it.
2. The poem is very beautiful, but could it be said to be naive or impractical? Why do you think people talk about '*falling* in love'?
3. Read 'The Nymph's Reply to the Shepherd', by Sir Walter Raleigh.

'THE PASSIONATE ASTRONAUT TO HIS LOVE', GREG SMENDA (NO. 70)
This is a parody of Marlowe's poem.

> A PARODY is a composition in which an author's style characteristics are ridiculed by imitation.

1. What style characteristics are imitated here?
2. Study how the comic effect is produced. For example: notice the flat, common, even vulgar sounds of 'mate' and 'spate' in the first verse. Contrast this with Marlowe's poetic 'love' and 'prove'. Is this effect repeated elsewhere?

'THE THICKNESS OF ICE', LIZ LOXLEY (NO. 71)
THE POEM
1. What experience is the poet describing here?
2. Is this like your own experience of friendship?
3. Do you think the extended metaphor of the poem works well?
4. Someone once said: 'You can write well about love only after you have fallen out of it'. Do you think that is true about this poet?

'LADY DIAMOND', UNKNOWN (NO. 72)

Notes

of muckle scorn – who was much ridiculed
to greet – to weep
stays – corsets
hinney – honey

DRAMA

1. After you have heard the poem a number of times, divide into your groups of 4 or 5. Each group should choose a scene from the poem to present as a tableau or sculpture. Try to ensure that there is a variety of scenes representing the progress of the whole story. When preparing, read and re-read the verse and try to be as true as possible to the image and mood of the scene. Each group, in sequence, can then show their scene as a sculpture, tableau or freeze frame while the rest watch.
2. Show the tableaux again. This time, each figure can utter a statement, as the inner voice of the character, at that moment. Keep the make-believe and the silence. If the atmosphere breaks, pause and begin again.
3. If you are really good at it, take the process a stage further. Perhaps the teacher, or a confident student, can play the role of a medium in contact with the spirits of the figures in the drama. This person can ask questions about the events shown . . . and the spirits from the tableaux can reply.
4. Finish with a round: Each student gets to make one unchallenged statement about the poem, beginning with 'I liked . . .' or 'I noticed that . . .'.
5. Read the poem again. Did the drama help you to understand it better? What did you learn?

This poem is in the form of a ballad. The BALLAD was one of the earliest forms of story poem. Many of these early ballads handed down to us are anonymous and were spoken or sung rather than written down. In the nineteenth and twentieth centuries, many poets adapted and developed the ballad in written form. Now, of course, there are also many modern sung ballads. See pages 168–69.

Most ballads have a number of common characteristics:
(a) They are narratives. In other words, they tell a story which is usually very dramatic.
(b) The most common themes dealt with are death, love and war.
(c) The language is usually simple and they often are written in simple four-line stanzas.
(d) The descriptions are often very colourful, with striking images.
(e) The lines rhyme and the poem usually has a lively beat or rhythm to carry the story along at a good pace.
(f) Often, there is dramatic dialogue.
(g) Sometimes there is a repeated refrain or chorus.

THE POEM
6. How many of the common characteristics of the ballad can you find in 'Lady Diamond'?
7. Rhythm: Can you work out how many stressed syllables there are in each line? Read it aloud. Can you name the metre? See pages 134–5.

'WOMAN IS', ROBIN MORGAN (NO. 73)
1. How many of the ideas/sentiments set out by Robin Morgan can you identify with? Explain.
2. Write a short story based on any one section.
3. Compose a voice poem (a 6 to 10 line speech, written in the 1st person) for any character featured in a section. Without comment, read them aloud, in rotation.
4. Debate the motion: 'That boys and girls see the world differently'.

'THE IDEAL HUSBAND', HARRY GRAHAM (NO. 74)
THE POEM
1. Write two paragraphs on the tone of this poem.
2. Comment on the rhymes.

'WHEN YOU ARE OLD', W.B. YEATS (NO. 75)
THE POEM
1. What is the poet describing here?
2. What does the poet want you to feel? Write two paragraphs on the mood or atmosphere of the poem.
3. What images do you find most effective? Why?

'GARDENING SUNDAY', BRIAN JONES (NO. 76)
'WHEN I'M SIXTY-FOUR', LENNON & McCARTNEY (NO. 77)
Which poem do you prefer? Why?

'YESTERDAY', PATRICIA POGSON (NO. 78)
Talk about this poem with your mother.

'SHALL I COMPARE THEE TO A SUMMER'S DAY?', WILLIAM SHAKESPEARE (NO. 79)
Notes:
   faire (1.7) – beauty   *untrim'd* (1.8) – stripped
   ow'st (1.10) – ownest, owns
THE POEM
1. What is the poet describing here?

> 2. The English or Shakespearean Sonnet is organised in three quatrains (four lines) and a rhyming couplet (two rhyming lines) – four sections or movements in all. Some poets, Shakespeare for one, used it to make three statements, followed by a conclusion.

What is the main point Shakespeare develops in each quatrain and what is his conclusion?
3. Can you now express the theme of the poem in two paragraphs?
4. What do you think of the metaphor he uses to express his love?
5. If we call the end rhyme of the first line *a* and that of the second *b*, work out the rhyming scheme.
6. Was Shakespeare dyslexic? Enquire about the spelling.

'ONE DAY I WROTE HER NAME UPON THE STRAND', EDMUND SPENSER (NO. 80)

Notes

A Second Hand – a second time
Eek – also
Devise – design or plan
Assay – try
Quoth – said
(P.S. We cleaned up Spenser's spelling.)

THE POEM
1. What is the poet describing here?
2. Can you express the theme of the poem in one paragraph?
3. Do you find his imagery appropriate to the theme?
4. Trace his thoughts through each quatrain and the couplet.
5. Can you work out the interesting rhyming scheme? Notice how the couplets are linked by rhyme, so the reader is not aware of separate sections.

GROUP WORK
6. In your groups, discuss and list the characteristics, advantages and disadvantages of sonnets, as compared to other forms of poetry you have read. REPORT BACK.

SECTION F – BIRTH TO DEATH

Music Suggestions

'Abide with Me', (hymn)
'Alone Again, Naturally', Gilbert O'Sullivan
'Anach Chuain', (a lament)
'Don't Pay the Ferryman', Chris de Burgh
'Eleanor Rigby', The Beatles
'Evening Falls', Enya (Watermark Album)
'Veronica', Elvis Costello

Exploring the Poems

'MORNING SONG', SYLVIA PLATH (NO. 81)
THE POEM
1. What words or images catch your attention? Why?
2. What is the relationship between the mother and child? Discuss this.
DESCRIPTIVE WRITING
3. Write five descriptive paragraphs on the newborn child or any young baby you have seen.

'THE BABY', OGDEN NASH (NO. 82)
'MID-TERM BREAK', SEAMUS HEANEY (NO. 83)
GROUP WORK
In your groups, discuss what aspects of these poems should be noticed by every reader. REPORT BACK. Have a student act as class secretary to note down all the different points. Make a chart.

'THE IDENTIFICATION', ROGER McGOUGH (NO. 84)
DRAMA ROUND
After you have heard the poem a number of times, do a *round* – each student makes one unchallenged statement beginning: 'I noticed that . . .'.
List the main points on the board.

'SHE DWELT AMONG THE UNTRODDEN WAYS', WILLIAM WORDSWORTH (NO. 85)
What do you think the poet is writing about?

NOS 83-85
GROUPS

> An ELEGY is a song or poem of lamentation for the dead.

Consider the three poems together. What points of similarity and difference can you find? REPORT BACK.

'TO WAKEN AN OLD LADY', WILLIAM CARLOS WILLIAMS (NO. 86)
CREATIVE WRITING
Write a short poem in this style, on one of the following titles:
'Childhood is . . .'   'Youth is . . .'   'Adolescence is . . .'

'GOOD', R.S. THOMAS (NO. 87)
THE POEM
1. What is the poet describing here?
2. What images catch your attention? Comment.
3. There are many contrasts or opposites in the poem. Can you spot them? Why do you think the poet uses them?
4. What do you think the poet is saying about death?
5. Comment on the title.

'DEATH IN THE VILLAGE', GRAHAM HOUGH (NO. 88)
THE POEM
1. What do you think is happening in this poem?
2. What do you think the poet wants us to feel? Explain.
3. To what images do you react most strongly? Explain.
4. Listen to 'Evening Falls' by Enya (Watermark Album).

'LET ME DIE A YOUNGMAN'S DEATH', ROGER McGOUGH (NO. 89)
'CROSSING THE BAR', ALFRED, LORD TENNYSON (NO. 90)
1. Compare the attitudes to death in these two poems. Write three paragraphs about them.
2. Which poem do you prefer? Why?

'DO NOT GO GENTLE INTO THAT GOOD NIGHT', DYLAN THOMAS (NO. 91)
Dylan Thomas communicates his meaning in wild and wonderful images rather than in statements.
1. Can you find the meaning in these images? Write the statement you think he intends in each stanza.
2. What are your favourite lines? Why?

'FOR EVERYTHING THERE IS A SEASON', ECCLESIASTES 2 (NO. 92)
Read this piece and think about it. What verses mean most to you now?

SECTION G – WAR

Reading on the Theme: Novels
'All Quiet on the Western Front', Erich Maria Remarque
'How Many Miles to Babylon', Jennifer Johnston

'Diary of Anne Frank'
'I am David', Anne Holm
'Fair Stood the Wind for France', H.E. Bates
'The Endless Steppe', Esther Hautzig
'The Silver Sword', Ian Serraillier

Music Suggestions
'1812 Overture', Tchaikovsky
'Mars', from 'The Planets', by Holst
'Threnody for the Victims of Hiroshima', Penderetecki
'Revolutionary Polonaise', Chopin

Songs of Particular Wars
'Amhrán na bhFiann'
'Battle Hymn of the Republic'
'Colonel Bogey'
'Deutschland Uber Alles'
'It's a Long Way to Tipperary'
'Keep the Home Fires Burning'
'Lily Marlene'
'Over There'
'Roses are Blooming in Picardy'
'Rule Britannia'
'The Stars and Stripes'
'When Johnny Comes Marching Home'
'The White Cliffs of Dover'

Anti-war Ballads
'Arthur McBride'
'The Green Fields of France'
'High Germany'
'The Band Played "Walzing Matilda"'
'The Town I Loved So Well'

War Medley
'Disposable Heroes', Metallica
'Give Peace a Chance', John Lennon
'Goodnight Saigon', Billy Joel
'Hiroshima Nagasaki Russian Roulette', Christy Moore
'Imagine', John Lennon
'In the Army Now', Status Quo
'The Last Farewell', Roger Whittaker
'19 – The Final Story', Paul Hardcastle
'Remember the Brave Ones', Christy Moore
'Tomorrow Belongs to Me', from the film 'Cabaret'
'Two Tribes', Frankie Goes To Hollywood
'Unknown Soldier', The Doors
'War', Bruce Springsteen
'World War', The Cure

Exploring the Poems

From 'THE TÁIN', TRANSLATED BY THOMAS KINSELLA (NO. 93)
1. Having considered the extract, each student makes one statement beginning: 'I noticed that . . .'. No one can challenge your statement. It doesn't matter if someone has already said what you intended to say, say it anyway.
2. What attitude to war is expressed in this extract from 'The Táin'? Give examples to back up your view.

'THE BURIAL OF SIR JOHN MOORE AFTER CORUNNA', CHARLES WOLFE (NO. 94)

Notes
Billow – waves
Reck – heed or care about

GROUP READING
1. The aim is to give a good dramatic reading which catches the tone of the poem.
(a) First read it quietly a number of times. Find out the meaning of any strange words or other questions of interpretation.
(b) Each student quietly prepares to read all of it to the small group. In the margin, pencil reading directions to yourself. Example: loudly; softly; slowly etc. Underline words to be stressed. Mark // where you think a pause is needed.
(c) For full effect, each student reads the entire poem and then the group discusses the interpretation. Or you may do it one verse at a time.
(d) On the basis of that discussion, decide who will read which verse when the group is performing for the class.
Groups perform in turn.
2. Class Round beginning 'I noticed that . . .' or 'I liked the reading of verse number . . . because . . .'.
3. What attitude to death in war is portrayed in this poem? Write three paragraphs on this.
4. How would you describe the tone of the poem?
5. Compare this with the tone of 'Dulce et Decorum est' by Wilfred Owen, page 87.

'THE SOLDIER', RUPERT BROOKE (NO. 95)
'AN IRISH AIRMAN FORSEES HIS DEATH', W.B. YEATS (NO. 96)

GROUPS
List the similarities and differences you find in these poems.
Think of: speaker; main preoccupations of speaker; his motivation in each case; attitude to war; tone or feeling the poem creates; imagery; format and style etc. or anything else you notice.

'IN FLANDERS FIELDS', JOHN McCREA (NO. 97)

THE POEM
1. What is the poet describing here?
2. What does he want you to feel? Explain.
3. What images do you notice in particular? Why?
MIME AND READING
4. Can each group devise a mime or a sculpture to accompany a reading? One member of the group reads the poem.

'DULCE ET DECORUM EST', WILFRED OWEN (NO. 98)
Note:
> '*Dulce et decorum est –*   'It is sweet and proper
> *Pro patria mori*'   to die for the fatherland'
> from 'Odes' III (ii), by Horace

THE POEM
1. The first stanza describes the soldiers, after their period of service in the front-line trenches, retreating to a rest area. What does the poet want us to understand about their condition? Write three paragraphs on this.
2. Do you consider that the similes which Wilfred Owen uses are effective? Comment.
3. Do the sounds of the words carry the meaning? Consider 'sludge', for example. Comment on the sounds of other words.
4. What is the poet trying to describe in the second stanza?
5. What do the verbs contribute to the atmosphere?
6. Explain the contrasts around which the third stanza is built.
7. Comment on the graphic details here.
8. A poet sometimes uses irony to highlight the contrasts between the imagined situation and the real. Can you find any examples here?
9. Can you express the theme of this poem in one paragraph?

CREATIVE WRITING
10. Write a letter home to a relative, friend or girlfriend (as if you were one of the soldiers who has just reached the rest area).

'THE GENERAL', SIEGFRIED SASSOON (NO. 99)
THE POEM
1. Who or what is being satirised here?
2. How is the satire achieved? Consider irony and rhyme.

READING
3. You might like to dip into Siegfried Sassoon's 'Memoirs of an Infantry Officer'.

'MILITARY SERVICE', ELIZABETH JENNINGS (NO. 100)
Write a letter, explaining his dilemma, which the young recruit might send to his mother. Be faithful to his feelings in the poem.

'THE HERO', SIEGFRIED SASSOON (NO. 101)
Note:
> *Wicked Corner* – section of the trenches at the front.

THE POEM
1. Write down three questions you would like to ask about this poem.

GROUP DISCUSSION
2. List the three best war films you remember seeing. Give a brief outline of the plot and three reasons why you liked it in each case. REPORT BACK.

'DEAD GERMAN YOUTH', C.P.S. DENHOLM-YOUNG (NO.102)
THE POEM
1. What images did you notice most clearly in this poem? Explain why.
2. What does the poet want you to feel? Write two paragraphs on this.
3. Can you express the theme of this poem in one paragraph?

NOS 103-106
'Killed in Action', Juliette de Bairacli-Levy
'Shells', Wilfrid Gibson
'The Evacuee', R.S. Thomas
'Pigtail', Tadeusz Rózewicz

1. Read these four poems silently, a number of times. They all deal with the effect of war on people other than soldiers. Think about them.
2. Choose the one which appeals most to you. Prepare to read it to the class and speak (for about one minute) on why you chose it. You can script your speech, in paragraphs, if you wish, or just make heading notes.
3. If possible, hear all the speeches in sequence which are on a particular poem. Choose a secretary to record all the main points made about that poem and put them on a chart. Can the class add to it?

'EVEN HITLER HAD A MOTHER', HERBERT FARJEON (NO. 107)
'ICARUS ALLSORTS', ROGER McGOUGH (NO. 108)
1. 'The black humour of this poem makes it very effective as an anti-nuclear protest.' Comment.
2. Do you know any other anti-nuclear poems or songs? Discuss this in your groups and REPORT BACK.

'YOUR ATTENTION PLEASE', PETER PORTER (NO. 109)
Notes
   DEW – Direct Early Warning radar station.
   'Valley Forge' – American government defence supplies
THE POEM
1. What interests you about this poem?
2. Can you suggest *how* the poem is made to sound dramatic?

3. Are there sections or phrases you find ironic? Explain.
4. In your groups, discuss and practise the best way to read this poem aloud.
DRAMA
5. In your groups, devise, rehearse and perform a short improvised drama which might suggest itself from any scene or image in this poem.

SECTION H – THOUGHTS FOR TODAY
Reading on the Theme: Novels
'Across the Barricades', series, Joan Lingard
'The Chocolate War', Robert Cormier
'The Diddakoi', Rumer Godden
'Starry Night', series, Catherine Sefton
'The Turbulent Term of Tyke Tiler', Gene Kemp
'Under Goliath', Peter Carter
'Z for Zachariah', Robert C. O'Brien

Non-Fiction
'A Place Apart', Dervla Murphy
'Nan: The Life of an Irish Travelling Woman', Sharon Gmelch

Music Suggestions
'Belfast Child', Simple Minds
'Empty Hands', John Cougar Mellencamp
'Motorway Song', The Black Family
'The Times, They Are A'Changing', Bob Dylan
'Don't Worry, Be Happy', Bobby McFerrin
'Land of Confusion', Genesis
'Pride in the Name of Love', U2
'The Town I Loved so Well', Phil Coulter

Exploring the Poems

'FIVE WAYS TO KILL A MAN', EDWIN BROCK (NO. 110)
THE POEM (for group discussion)
1. What is the poet describing here? What do you consider to be the theme of this poem?
2. Would this piece be just as effective if written in prose paragraphs? Discuss.
3. What images from life in the 1980s or 1990s would you use to illustrate this theme? REPORT BACK.
CREATIVE WRITING
4. Write in paragraphs or verses about some of the images mentioned which you thought particularly striking.

'ONE IN TEN', UB40 (NO. 111)
THE LYRICS
1. With which issues of 20th century life does this deal?
2. What images do you particularly notice? Why?
CREATIVE WRITING
3. Write a poem beginning: 'I am one of the other nine . . .' and read it to the group or class.
4. Compose a protest song or ballad on any issue that moves you.

'GIRLS IN A FACTORY', DENIS GLOVER (NO. 112)
1. What images do you notice? Explain.
2. Find a picture which would illustrate this poem. Explain your choice.
3. Write the thoughts of a girl in the poem, as she might have written them into her diary.

'FILM STAR', IAN SERRAILLIER (NO. 113)
GROUP DISCUSSION
1. What does the poem suggest about the life of the film star? Do you think it is fair comment? Discuss and REPORT BACK.
WRITING
2. What do you consider to be the two major themes in this poem? Write a paragraph on each.

'ADMAN', NIGEL GRAY (NO. 114)
1. What does the poem suggest about the nature of advertising? Is this fair comment? Discuss.
2. Consider the effectiveness of the central metaphor in this poem.
3. Study some ads from newspapers, magazines, radio and TV. Consider the use of persuasive language. How does an ad catch your attention? Consider alliteration, assonance, rhyme, memorable jingle, catchy slogan, image etc.
4. Write a jingle or a slogan for a new shampoo; or a new ice cream; or new washing powder; or a personal stereo or any object you wish to sell.
5. Write an article, justifying your choices, on 'The Five Indispensable Objects in My Life' (other than food or clothes!).

'EXECUTIVE', JOHN BETJEMAN (NO. 115)
THE POEM
1. Is the lifestyle of the young executive extremely glamorous or is there a darker side to it?

2. Study the speech in the second verse. What exactly does the executive reveal about his job? Do you know any modern 'yuppie-speak'? Consider the jargon such as 'software', 'interface' etc. used about computers. Have you heard any of these words and phrases used in ordinary social conversations?
3. What do you think is the meaning of the last line?
4. How would you describe the tone of this poem – is it humourous, satirical, elegiac or what? Explain.

'HAPPINESS', CARL SANDBURG (NO. 116)
What themes are dealt with in this poem?

'CULTIVATORS', SUSAN TAYLOR (NO. 117)
THE POEM
1. What is the poet describing here?
2. Give your opinion of the metaphor in the first stanza.
3. What do you think is the meaning of the second stanza?
CREATIVE WRITING
4. Write a poem beginning: 'We, who work with mind and pen . . .' or any 'We, who work with . . .'.

'IN MY COUNTRY', PITIKA NTULI (NO. 118)
1. What does the poet feel in this poem? Explain.
2. Did you see the film 'Cry Freedom'? Listen to a tape of the sound track.

'GRANDPA', PAUL CHIDYAUSIKU (NO. 119)
THE POEM
1. What are the differences in attitudes and lifestyles between the poet and the new generation?
2. How do you think the poet feels towards the new generation?
Explain by reference to the text.
MEDIA
3. Interview a grandparent or any older person about the main changes which have occurred in society since they were young. Record the interview and REPORT BACK.

'WHAT IS A PROTESTANT, DADDY?', PAUL DURCAN (NO. 120)
THE POEM
1. What images spring to the poet's mind when he recalls how he, as a child, thought of Protestant clergymen? What do these images suggest?
2. Does he still feel that way? Explain.

CREATIVE WRITING
3. Write a short poem beginning: 'What is a Catholic, Daddy?'.
PUBLIC SPEAKING
4. Working in groups, research some information on the other religions to be found in Ireland today. Present that information to the class.

'FROM THE IRISH', JAMES SIMMONS (NO. 121)
THE POEM
1. What is the poet describing here?
2. Comment on the appropriateness of the similes in lines 5 and 6. What is the effect?
3. What does the poet want us to feel? Explain.
4. What do you think is his attitude to the bomber? Comment on the tone of lines 1, 9 and 10.

'MISSIONARY', D.M. THOMAS (NO. 122)
DRAMA
It might be interesting to consider the poem as a narrative voice for a classroom drama. One student, or the teacher, could read the text and various groups could devise improvised scenes, mimes or tableaux to illustrate and extend passages or images from it.
1. Small groups could consider what scenes best lend themselves to improvisation. For example, you could have: a mime for entry to earth; various voices describing the scenes during the 'agonisingly slow descent towards the village'; scenes involving real people and conversations for the 'into the village, into the houses, inns' section; the newborn baby scene; scenes of his youth; scenes to illustrate 'the more I spoke . . .' sections; scene for 'in the end I tried too hard . . .'; the conversation of Thoorin and his friends on their return journey; and a final scene. But you can work up any scenes you like.
2. Rehearse in groups. Then perform the dramatised reading.
3. Finish with a round of 'I noticed about the poem . . .'.
4. Look up the meaning of the word ALLEGORY. Could this poem be seen to be an allegory in any way? List the points of similarity.

'LET IT BE', LENNON AND McCARTNEY (NO. 123)
Listen to it or sing it.

'GOD'S GRANDEUR', GERARD MANLEY HOPKINS (NO. 124)
Notes:
Reck His Rod – heed his authority
Seared – made incapable of feeling
Bleared – made watery or inflamed

THE POEM
1. Look up the meaning of the word 'grandeur'. Of the many meanings, which do you think best applies here?
2. To what does Hopkins compare the grandeur of God? What do the two similes used in the first 3 lines suggest about this? Are they expected comparisons? Comment.
3. What effect does growing industrialisation have on the world, according to Hopkins (lines 4–8)?
4. How do the words carry the poet's attitude? Consider 'have trod, have trod' and the Anglo-Saxon words 'Seared, bleared, smeared'. Consider also the sounds of 'trod' and 'shod' and the effect of alliteration in the poem.
5. Is the sestet full of hope for the world? Explain
6. How is the sense of excitement communicated? Consider the syntax (the placing or order of words in the line) – example: 'springs' in line 12. Consider also the effect of the exclamations in lines 12 and 14.
7. Read the last line for sounds alone and see how they run up the register or scale from the heavy vowels of 'world' and 'brood', through 'war' and 'bre' to the high notes of 'bright wings'. This is what Hopkins called *vowelling off* (as opposed to the use of same sounds or assonance, which he called *vowelling on*).
8. What do you think of the image of the Holy Ghost in the sestet?
9. Consider all the images used to describe God. Do they have anything in common?
10. Examine how Hopkins uses the sounds of words in general. Which alliteration do you think works best? Look at the intricate and unusual patterns of the last line. Which onomatopoeia works best?
11. Look at the structure and rhyming scheme of the sonnet.

'DESIDERATA', MAX EHRMANN (NO. 125)

Think about this. Then write a poem or a story beginning: 'You are a child of the universe, no less than the trees and the stars'.

or

Write an essay on the title: 'With all its sham, drudgery and broken dreams, it is still a beautiful world'.